I0434526

Waiting for the New Führer

Waiting for the New Führer

✦

The German Euro-Apartheid

Analysis of German strategies
"They are marching again"

Ralph T. Niemeyer

iUniverse, Inc.
New York Lincoln Shanghai

Waiting for the New Führer
The German Euro-Apartheid

iUniverse, Inc.

For information address:
iUniverse, Inc.
2021 Pine Lake Road, Suite 100
Lincoln, NE 68512
www.iuniverse.com

ISBN: 0-595-29552-5 (pbk)

ISBN: 0-595-66015-0 (cloth)

Printed in the United States of America

Contents

The Germans finally have achieved economically what Hitler failed to achieve by military terrorism and brutal violence against all peoples of this planet...
(RTN)

Again, Social Democrats will say that
they had only prevented the worst.
-Kurt Tucholsky-

Instead of a Foreword

Once discredited by it's blunt and deliberate betrayal of their voters, the Schröder-led "Social Democratic" government will be buried in the cemetery of the other "socialist-, labour- and social-democratic, green or reform-communist" protagonists of their kind who pretended too much while committing to a crackdown on social policy, human and civil rights and the environment. Their liberal and right-wing predecessors would not have dared to execute these policies, as they feared resistance by unions, environmentalists and civil rights activists, but also by the ordinary citizens who will wake up by then and vote for a charismatic leader who appears modern, tough but just, and who will use his charm in order to cover up the fact that in reality he is promoting chauvinism, nationalism and right-wing ideology. By allowing this to happen, every thinking person is as much responsible as future victims of that movement who don't speak or cry out now, as we are still able to do so, and say 'No', loud and clear.

1

Germany's Long-term EU Strategy

1. Germany and its neighbors

What is it our fellow European neighbors suspect that we Germans are ready to commit to? Where does the fear come from when French columnists write about the predominance of the Germans? Why were the French, especially, so reluctant in 1989 to allow us to be unified ultimately under one statehood after painful and long separation by a barbaric border? What does the term "German problem" imply, and why is it still used today, almost sixty years after World War II? Are we young Germans responsible for the crimes two generations before us committed? How can we contribute to permanent peace and equilibrium in the world, and do we have a special moral obligation whether or not we want to feel responsible for Auschwitz and whether or not there is such a thing as collective guilt, which even my generation has been taught about in school in a way that made many of us feel a burden of the past, and let many of us behave differently when meeting fellow students from France, Poland and Britain. There are many questions, but I think we have to put the "German problem" into context, as it is there and can not be ignored. First, one has to consider that Germany is surrounded by nine neighbors, of which Poland and France would be the larger and more powerful nations who therefore have been seen as rivals by all German governments since 1871 (the first German unification). Moreover, the Pan-European corridors all begin in or go through Germany. Those corridors have their roots in the Middle Ages. The most vital corridors are the so-called fourth corridor, leading from Berlin and Dresden to Istanbul via Prague, Bratislava, Gyor, Budapest, Arad, Krajova, Sofia and Plovdiv, with some ramifications with Nuremberg, Vienna, Bucharest and Constanza; the eighth corridor, from the Albanian port of Durres to Warna in Bulgaria via Tirana, Kaftan, Skopje, Deve Bair, Sofia, Plovdiv and Burgas, and the tenth corridor, connecting Salzburg, Ljubljana, Zagreb, Belgrad, Nis, Skopje, Veles and Thessaloniki. Ramifications connect this corridor to Graz, Maribor, Sofia, Bitola, Florina and Igoumenitza, as well as Augsburg. It has always been the vital strategic interest of all German governments to secure these corridors, as Germany's trade and economy needed them for the transport routes as well as for possible expansion into other territorries.

One can say Germany is in the heartland of Europe, and the geopolitical consequences have led to two world wars. It is important for any analysis of present German strategy to understand that the two world wars were not triggered because of one evil Kaiser or Fuehrer who was angry at neighboring nations or simply crazy, as many historians still want to make us believe when they write about the evil genom of Hitler, but because of economic interests leading to German imperialism at a time all other major European powers already had their share of the cake in their colonies, which Germany almost completely missed, because of its failure to unite some three hundred German states, principalities and micro kingdoms. As Germany has always been a major economic power in Europe, lacking any dependencies and access to raw materials and resources abroad, its economy was and is constantly suffering from an expansion crisis. As Germany could make use of its geographic advantages only when controlling the transport routes from and through its own territory, it would logically also attempt to secure its grip on other routes that have vital meaning for its own expansion. It is, of course, in the German interest to establish and wherever possible own or otherwise control the Pan-European routes or corridors. By controlling those it would be the dominate power on the continent, to have access to and make use of the Pan-European Network (PAN), which has many more global effects that we may now be able to explain. The network is designed to develop the former Soviet Union and other East European "emerging markets." It is, of course, essential to integrate these new markets into the European economic system, not for the sake of their economies, but for the sake of our, German, expansion. So far, the European Union has advanced this quite efficiently, given that the EU pursued this only since the early nineties.

The full scale will be implemented once the pan-European transport system (PETRA) covers the area from the Atlantic to the Urals as well as the EU-associated Mediterranean of the Maghreb, an economic area of more than one billion people, 18,000 kilometers of roads, 20,000 kilometers of railways, thirty-eight airports, thirteen seaports, forty-nine rivers, numerous gas and oil pipelines, as well as telecommunication knots.

Up to now the EU has invested more than 90 billion Euros in this venture, which has been pursued again and again since Charles the Great, but suffered heavy backlashes every single time the capitalistic expansion led to wars and even world wars.

Since Germany accounts for the largest gross national product (GNP), and since incorporating the GDR, is the most populous country in the EU, it asked for more votes in the council of ministers at the Nice Summit in December, 2000. However, this has proved a bad idea, at least in terms of timing. First of all, the European Parliament reflects the population of member countries by a proportional representation, while the council of ministers deals on inter-governmental levels. Secondly, it did not appear to be wise to get too pushy on this issue. The International Herald Tribune stated on 7 December, 2000, that "The 'German problem' antedates World War I. It is not just an affair of Nazism and WW II; it goes back to the Franco-Prussian war and German unification in 1871. When Bismarck brought all but Austria undessa's domination, the German state was the most populous in

Europe. It was too big. It unbalanced the old Europe, overshadowing France and Austria-Hungary, and challenging the British Empire."[1]

That's exactly where we stand again, after two world wars and the cold war being over, by neither side carrying a permanent victory. All Adenauer and de Gaulle negotiated in 1951 was about coal and steel, but in fact it was more, it was about the new equilibrium in Europe. It laid the ground for increasing cooperation, first economically, then politically, and it did not take long until one spoke of the French-German brotherhood and that it was a driving force for the unification of Europe. All these decades it had been essential to the few European nations being involved, that all members be treated as equals, no matter what size or how populous. This was the euqilibrium that made the French, Dutch, Belgians and Luxemburgers gain confidence in the new Germany. Having suffered tremendously from previous German expansions, those nations have been very wary of any attempt by the Germans to fall back into hegemonial power behavior. It probably helped at this stage that Germany was divided and not sovereign. The two Germanies were rivals from the very beginning, and the East Germans, claiming higher moral standing for being tougher on NAZIs, may also have been responsible by their sheer existence for a more socially balanced—and in its foreign affairs modest—West Germany, claiming to represent all of Germany. In fact, this Germany was the one the world may have liked better, as it was a non-repressive, liberal society, abstaining not only because of the cold war but also because of a general mood in Germany from any military adventurism and advocating a modest foreign policy—at least publicly.

All this changed after 3rd October, 1990, and the promises of Chancellor Kohl and Foreign Minister Genscher that, "Only peace shall come from German soil" were soon forgotten. The Herald Tribune noted that "Germany's venture into policy leadership in 1992, by forcing EU recognition of Croatia and Slovenia, did not prove a good idea."[2]

---

1.   International Herald Tribune (IHT) 7th December 2000

To put it mildly, other European leaders were not impressed by Foreign Minister Hans Dietrich Genscher combining German approval of the Maastricht accord with a European vote on its policy towards the new—old—Yugoslavian republics, who were about to trigger the first war in Europe since 1945. Should the agreement signed at Maastricht survive only the following days it would be necessary for Europe to speak with a single voice in the emerging Balkan conflict, meaning that Chancellor Kohl's promise of "full diplomatic recognition for Croatia and Slovenia before Christmas" [3] would be honored in exchange for the German's willingness to 'sacrifice' their beloved Deutschemark to the ECU, later EURO, single currency project, which they advocated more than any other European Nation. Even the traditionally German-friendly Turkish Foreign Ministry's Balkan expert, Alev Kilic, asserted that the early diplomatic recognition Croatia and Slovenia,won by the EC following intense German pressure, buried any hope for a peaceful solution in the Balkan conflict.[4]

Even the liberal weekly DIE ZEIT admitted that "the splitting-up of the Yugoslavian state, along with the closer alignment of the Croats and Slovenians with the German economy, brought kind of an emancipation of these peoples who were previously attached to the empires in central Europe and later with the 'Third Reich', but also was meant to be a punishment for the Serbs, who have been on the victor's side in both world wars. And thirdly, it made those treaties vanish, which punished Germany for its two defeats. In short: due to the almighty economy, Germany regained what it lost in battle."

It was terrible for the German government under Helmut Kohl that Secretary of State Warren Christopher openly criticized the government in Bonn and made German foreign policy responsible for the catastrophy in Bosnia-Herzegovina. Christopher said in an interview with USA TODAY: "All the process of granting diplomatic recogni-

---

2.   International Herald Tribune (IHT) 7th December 2000
3.   Deutscher Bundestag 15th December 1991
4.   Frankfurter Allgemeine Zeitung (FAZ)25th February 1992

tion to Croatia and Slovenia contained serious mistakes, and the Germans bear a special responsibility for that. My government was not in power at the time in question, but all our experts agree that the problems we are facing today in Bosnia-Herzegovina stem from the recognition of Croatia, and later Bosnia."

This was definitely the first rift between the trans-Atlantic partners, and it reflects the anger the American administration felt over the German emancipation. Of course, it would be naive to assume that the Americans were really worried about the atrocities committed in the civil war in the former Yugoslavia, but it was the new rivalry with Germany, which re-entered the international arena as a sovereign and independent nation, though still morally burdened by its past. Especially, the criticism of the French foreign minister, Roland Dumas, saying that "the responsibility of Germany and the Vatican regarding the acceleration of the Yugoslavian conflict would be enormous," weighs heavy. All foreign signatory parties to the Two Plus Four Treaty over German unification disapproved the united Germany's first steps on the international stage. The Americans especially seemed to be at odds with the new German foreign policy. The International Herald Tribune commented that Germany had claimed "policy leadership in 1992, by forcing EU recognition of Croatia and Slovenia,"which "did not prove a good idea". And the IHT commentators put this into context with Germany's grip on EU leadership: "Neither did its insistence that the Netherlands' Wim Duisenberg become head of the European Central Bank. The international takeover ambitions of German banks have led to recent humiliations. The re-dynamized German stock market failed in its attempt this year to link up with the London stock market and create a pan-European stock exchange. Daimler Benz's takeover of Chrysler looks like ending in fiasco…"

Each of these facts may not have any major impact on the course of history, but it nevertheless shows how Germany pushes itself forward and that it should be more careful with this, as might other nations who realize that Germany is advancing to be the powerhouse of

Europe, not only economically, but also in terms of strategy and hegemony lead to reject such dominance. It might have been acceptable to most European countries that Germany was claiming to have a right to at least partly get rid of its past, not to be reminded of the holocaust over and over again, but it has been the German chancellors, Kohl and Schröder, who emphasized the leadership role Germany was seeking. Chancellor Kohl said at a party convention of the CDU in Dresden on 17th December, 1991, "that the fact that Croatia and Slovenia will be diplomatically recognized in January, 1992, was a major diplomatic policy achievement for Germany."[5]

Former U.S. Secretary of State Henry A. Kissinger, himself a dubious figure on the diplomatic stage when it comes to hidden agendas in order to undermine democratically elected governments, instead said in 1996 that the early recognition of the independent former Yugoslavian republics, especially in the case of Bosnia-Herzegovina, did not create a new state but provoked a new civil war.[6] At least in his analysis, Kissinger is unbeatable.

Nowadays it raises major concern if one no less than the present Chancellor Gerhard Schröder is quoted by the New York Times saying that, "Germany calls itself a great power"…again, we wish to add. In this article[7] Schröder departs from post-war political correctness in speaking openly of the self-interest the German people have and will pursue, and thus lays a new vision of the international role Germany intends to play in due course. This new openess is seen by the New York Times as a signal to end formally Germany's self-imposed reserve since 1945, and as departing from Chancellor Kohl and all predecessors in studiously avoiding any reference to Germany as "great power" or to national self-interest. The arrival of a post-war-born generation in power as well as the move of the federal government from Bonn to Berlin also marks a policy shift, as the NYT commentator Roger

---

5.   deutsche presse agentur (dpa) 17th December 1991
6.   Die Welt, 8th September 1996
7.   New York Times, (NYT/IHT) 13th September 1999

Cohen writes. Remarkable also is the chancellor's quotation: "NATO used to be an organization that served to protect Germany, but also as protection against Germany…this concept has no value from now on." In its place, Schröder suggests, a Germany without complexes has emerged. Colleague Cohen asserts that although Germany does not own nuclear weapons, it still may be seen as a great power, not only economically, but also militarily, as the seventy-eight-day bombing of Yugoslavia over the Kosovo-conflict in which "Germany played a prominent role" (NYT) signaled an end of the German postwar principle that only "peace shall go out from German soil." Unfortunately, many Germans feel that Germany has paid its dues, is a good neighbor and partner for the other European nations and even generous in allowing them to participate in the single currency project, EURO, which Germans have been overwhelmingly hostile to, as they feel they are sacrificing their beloved deutschemark, symbol of resurrection out of ruins and the economic boom after the war. It is this issue that can be watched being debated furiously and emotionally rather than logically, and not the debate about peace and war. Once the German media had portrayed the then Yugoslavian President Milosevic as a barbaric butcher, the mood in Germany that one protect human rights and even intervene militarily to let "Auschwitz never happen again," as the former pacifist and now neo-liberal Foreign Minister Joseph Fischer relentlessly and painfully repeated again and again, gained ground. No matter that there has never been any proof for the allegations, and only a few German journalists dared to ask why there has been no footage of the concentration camps Fischer and former Defense Minister Scharping were believed to have seen there. It was too damned easy to sell this story of the bad Serbs and good Croats and Slovenians and poor and surpressed Kosovo Albanians to the German people. They were only rarely interested. The feeling prevailed that Germany really has paid its dues and should play a "normal" role on the international stage, whatever this would involve.

But Germany still was held back by its constitution, as well as the so-called "Two Plus Four" Treaty on German unification, dated 12th September, 1990. Article 26 of the basic law, our constitution, clearly prohibits any aggressive act: "Actions designed to interfere and carried out with the intention to interfere with the peaceful coexsistence of the peoples, especially the launching of a war of aggression, are unconstitutional, and have to be prosecuted as a felony." Moreover, the German criminal code[8] defines "Whoever prepares the launching of a war of aggression (referencing article 26, paragraph one of the basic law) into which the Federal Republic of Germany may be drawn, faces life in prison, with a minimum sentence of ten years without parole."

One would think that this is strong enough to prevent any government from acting like the present Red-Green government under Schröder and Fischer does. However, it appears that the German major industries, banks, corporations and their shareholders *need* the "pacifist" Greens and "Social-Democratic" SPD to carry out and deliver what Helmut Kohl's government didn't even dare to do: brutal destruction of the once-celebrated West German system of a social free market society, a tax reform shunning middle class entrepreneurs, while shuffling billions over billions into the hands of the owners of Deutsche Bank, Daimler Chrysler, Siemens and virtually any of the thirty Dax-listed major holdings, as well, of course, as leading Germany into its new international role, raising fears of a renewed nationalism, militarism and a Germany-above-all attitude that would have caused an uprising among the then-oppositional Greens and Social Democrats, who most likely would have joined the once-powerful unions and formed some resistance if the conservative government of chancellor Kohl had even thought about this.

Yes, it had to be a Green party, with its roots in anti-militarism and anti-nuclear power movements, to lead Germany with its Foreign Minister Joseph Fischer into the first war after WWII. Somehow one can not rule out that some of the Greens really believed that Germany's

---

8.   § 80 (StGB) German Criminal Code

engagement in the Balkan wars was purely humanitarian-driven, but how naive does one have to be not to see the propaganda tools used in order to convince party members who were told that they had to prevent Auschwitz from happening again?

We should leave this aspect aside for a moment and concentrate on the mere legal aspects of the German involvement and possible intentions when having their grip on the new world order after 11th September, 2001, whoever really planned and executed this act of terrorism. First of all, the Red-Green government disregarded existing law and international treaties, such as the so-called Two Plus Four treaty, of which article two clearly states that, "The governments of the Federal Republic of Germany and the German Democratic Republic emphasize herewith that only peace shall come from German soil. As per the constitution of the unified Germany, all action which may be intended to disturb the peaceful living together and coexistence of the peoples are unconstitutional and prosecuted as a felony. The governments of the Federal Republic of Germany and the German Democratic Republic herewith declare that the unified Germany will never ever use its weapons except in accordance with the charter of the United Nations." The socalled "Kosovo war," NATO's seventy-eight-day air campaign against an independent, sovereign state, winner of the Second World War, cold-war ally of both, East and West, member and founding nation of the United Nations, the Federal Republic of Yugoslavia, had at no stage ever won the approval of the United Nations Security Council, and therefore has been illegal, especially in terms of German participation. Such participation was especially delicate if one takes Germany's history into consideration, it having fought two wars in the past hundred years against Serbia. One should think that no matter what problems Yugoslavia had and who caused them, Germany would abstain from any intervention merely on the grounds of its own history, its dark past, especially concerning earlier involvements in the Balkans. Moreover, German law did not allow the government of Schröder and Fischer to participate in any way in the NATO war against the Federal Republic of Yugoslavia. The German basic law, our constitution, goes even further: it calls such action committed by Schröder, Scharping and Fischer a war of aggression.[9] Especially, the absence of a UN mandate (as demanded by the Two plus Four Treaty) is a slap in the face to people who suffered from German nationalism, NAZISM, military terrorism and torture. Furthermore, article 87a of the basic law clearly states that "except for defense, the German bundeswehr may be used only in accordance with the regulations of this basic law." The character of military operations ordered by the Schröder government were clearly not defensive.

2. A Chancellor and the Opportunity of the Moment

The aftermath of the events of 11th September, 2001, also provide rising legal questions. It does not make a difference whether the U.S. administration of President-in-charge Bush emotionally feels obliged to wage a war against Afganistan because someone (history will eventually be able to determine whether this attack really came from abroad or whether it has been rightists or fascists like the Aryan Action Group who blew up the Oklahoma City Building, a fact that has never been fully investigated) destroyed the World Trade Center skyscrapers on 11th September, 2001. Nothing would make a retaliation carried out by the United States of America legal, especially since the secret services had concrete knowledge since 1995 of attacks to be carried out by hijacked planes targeting the World Trade Center in New York, Sears Tower in Chicago and CIA headquarters in Langley, according to Der Spiegel.[10] No matter what, the administration under President-in-charge Bush commits crimes by retaliating in breach of existing international law. Therefore, the Schröder government is confronted with serious accusations, ranging from criminal charges, namely the launching of a war of aggression,[11] coinciding with the foundation of a crimi-

---

9. Article 26, Basic Law, 29th May 1949
10. Spiegel online 7th December 2001

nal, possibly terrorist gang,[12] high treason against the federation,[13] to possible charges on grounds of crimes committed against humanity, which may have to be investigated at a later stage.

Following the terrorist attack of 11th September, 2001, in New York and Washington, Schröder was eager to declare the German Federal Government's "unlimited solidarity" with the United States of America. Furthermore, he offered military support without being asked for it, and despite the fact that no evidence has been presented pointing to a particular terrorist organisation, group or gang being responsible for the terrorist attack. It has also not been clear whether or not the terrorists carried out their attacks from abroad. In fact, this would not be an issue of controversy, as article 5 of the NATO treaty is based on the UN Charter, which clearly declares that only such armed attacks that have been carried out by a state may justify military response. Since NATO's foundation is legally based on article 51 of the UN Charter, the terrorist attacks of 11th September, 2001, do not constitute an attack from a state and can not legally create a state of defense for the United States of America and/or its allies. Therefore, invoking article 5 of the NATO treaty has been an unlawful misinterpretation. Schröder nevertheless agreed to such an undertaking.

Moreover, Schröder publically claimed that NATO's decision was based on the United Nation's Security Council Resolution of 12th September, 2001. This, in fact, would be evidence against his case, as this resolution only mentions a terrorist attack and not an armed military attack, which indeed would be the principal requirment to justify any counterattack backed by article 51 of the UN Charter. The United States of America failed to win agreement for the wording of the resolution to be amended or changed on 28th September, 2001, which would have made it possible to declare a state of defense.

---

11. felony, § 80 and 80a StGB Criminal Code lifelong imprisonment
12. felony, § 129, resp. §129 a (StGB)
13. § 81a (StGB)

Therefore, the war against Afghanistan and possibly other target countries has been simply illegal due to misinterpretation of the UN Resolution dated 12th September, 2001, and unlawful interpretation of article 5 of the NATO treaty.

German Defense Minister at that time, Rudolf Scharping, is said to have urged a military response,[14] and Schröder has claimed to have brought the European governments to speak with a single voice and accept Germany's new leadership role.[15] However, the government of the United States of America has not asked for any military support, although Schröder, Scharping and Fischer always maintained that this was the case.

This culminated in Schröder claiming that the U.S. government had asked on 6th November, 2001, for such military support, even the deployment of ground troops. Senior U.S. government officials promptly denied issuing such a request. and emphasized that "the German and Italian governments have been pressing Washington to respond to offers of military assistance made immediately after 11th September, 2001." [16]

It appears that the United States of America and Great Britain did not want to have any allied 'support' from Germany or any other state when making their way through to the Oil of the Caspian Sea. A senior U.S. strategist in the Pentagon, David Trucker, explained on 16th October, 2001, that "there is only one region for the U.S. worth fighting for: the Persian Gulf, Caspian Sea and Central Asia, as seventy-five per cent of the world's oil reserves and thirty-three per cent of the natural gas reserves are to be located there."[17] And if Schröder, Scharping and Fischer only read the paper they would know about a U.S. energy consortium's plan to lay a pipline from central Asian Turkmenistan through Afghanistan to the Indian Ocean.[18]

---

14. Financial Times 17th September 2001
15. International Herald Tribune 20th September 2001
16. International Herald Tribune 7th November 2001
17. Tageszeitung 16th October 2001

The German government is probably afraid not to be able to justify their dubious aims publicly. It only makes it worse that Schröder, Scharping and Fischer not only *offer* military assistance but also <u>press</u> the U.S. to accept such participation in their brutal and barbaric war, employing cluster bombs, the ultimate conventional force, against mainly civilians.

Paragraph 80 (StGB) of the German criminal code declares that whoever prepares or launches a war of aggression in which the Federal Republic of Germany may be drawn faces life-long imprisonment.

The character of military operations ordered by the government were clearly not defensive and contradict not only the German constitution and German law but also the UN Charter, international treaties and UN resolutions. The combined commitment of several accused of executing such orders constituting a crime culminates in the definition as per the German criminal code §129 a (StGB) as a criminal and terrorist gang. The fact that Schröder, Scharping and Fischer held public offices undermines the integrity and authority of the institutions of the Federal Republic of Germany, and are to be seen as high treason against the federation (§ 81a StGB).

Finally, the use of the term "empower" (ermächtigen) in the draft legislation, to enable the government to execute military action in an undefined area, suggests that there is some connotation regarding the fact that this term has not been legally used in Germany for any government action since 1933. The cabinet release, dated 7th November, 2001, says: "The federal minister of defense herewith will be *empowered* to commit troops to participate in the operation 'enduring freedom' after constitutional authorization by the German Bundestag".

The Schröder government intended to use this "Ermächtigungsgesetz" (law of empowerment) to become a party in an illegal war. Parts of the German media helped the gang of Schröder, Scharping and Fischer to cover up the real reasons for this war. The daily Handelsblatt[19] suggested that, "so far Mr. Schröder has managed to make

18. Wirtschaftswoche 04th October 2001

the development appear inevitable, although it is the responsibility of the German federal government, who indeed has become pushy."

And this is what the German government really had to do if it wanted to have a say in the future of Afghanistan and the entire region rich in oil and gas reserves. The Americans were quite reluctant to let anyone else, except for the British, whose BP gasoline giant is part of the BP-AMOCO venture, participate in their adventurous undertakings to secure their grip on Caspian Sea resources. However, the EU under German leadership was able to circumvent U.S.-led military efforts by a coup-like secret agenda, unraveling when inviting Afghan exile groups to Bonn into the German government's Petersberg guest house. The U.S. had to watch how Germany guided the Afghan rivals to a multi-party government. Of course, this did not happen without a major economic boost from the EU, which held its conference on financial aid to Afghanistan the same afternoon in Berlin. Thus, the EU and Germany secured their influence in the postwar Afghanistan and even found a minister-president, Karzai, a former oil man for Unocal, for the country, whom the U.S. had objected to and probably attempted to kill by a bomb that left him slightly hurt, but killed three of their own soldiers in a "tragic accident." From the very beginning the U.S. supported the old king, and hoped that once its military ambitions had succeeded he would be an easy-to-cope-with partner in the postwar Afghani government, refraining from posing any demands in connection with the pipeline projects of Chevron-Texaco and BP-AMOCO. As the U.S. was eager to keep Germany out of Afghanistan, it was shunned by the Bonn conference, where Afghani groups were calling for an international force led by Germany.[20] They had to make good on this field by increasing their presence, but somehow failed, as New York Times correspondent Nicholas D. Kristof noted in the International Herald Tribune,[21] saying that the diplomats among his

---

19. Handelsblatt, 6th November 2001
20. Frankfurter Allgemeine Zeitung (FAZ) 30th November 2001
21. IHT 8th Decmeber 2001

countrymen were "conspicuously absent" in Kabul, while the Europeans were already there, busy opening their embassies.

And colleague Kristof also noted that Afghanis were longing for security, which "yet, incredibly, the Bush administration initially not only refused to provide…in Kabul, but also blocked the Europeans from sending in troops." And he went on, applauding the EU for taking the initiative: "Fortunately, European diplomats outmaneuvered the Americans in Bonn, and Washington is being forced to acquiesce in a modest number of foreign troops in the Kabul area."

Headlines of U.S. papers a couple of days before the terrorist attack of 11th September, 2001, read like this: "Americans blame Bush on Economy",[22] or "Bush worried about Economy and Boy, he has reason to."[23].What most people have not realized is that the American economy has not only been hit by a "slowdown" as most commentators always maintained, but by a sharp recession, dwindling down to a depression. The IHT published an editorial on 12th September, 2001, while the editorial must have been written well before that date. It was headlined: "Panic over Economy." Well, what was the situation before 11th September, 2001?

Here are some facts:

---

22. New York Times, 10th September 2001
23. San Francisco Chronicle 8th September 2001

2

International Implications

1. The American Dream...

When Alan Greenspan decided to lower the interest rate on 3rd January, 2001, NASDAQ rose the very same day by 14.2 per cent, and produced the biggest-ever growth within a day in its history. The value of all American stocks rose by 700 billion U.S. dollars. But only a day later, everything was back to normal again. And when Greenspan lowered interest rates again by half a per cent each time in February and March of the same year, the stocks even tumbled into a kind of mini-recession, and nothing like a phenomenal growth could be stimulated. Greenspan's tools were losing their power.

In the last decade of the twentieth century, the amount of money invested daily on international markets reached an unprecedented and unbelievable four trillion U.S. dollars. Even more is spent every day in trading stocks and derivatives. The Hausse of the nineties has solely been financed by these virtual funds, which although not backed by economic output or real production, indeed have some significant influence on the real economy. In monetary theory, this would mean direct and permanent inflation. The fact that this is not the case proves that inflation itself is not primarily a monetary problem but one of real fights about ownership and distribution of wealth.

Excessive creation of virtual funds does not necessarily lead to significant increase in demand for goods and services. Whether or not this unreal and excessive creation of virtual funds really affects the demand

17

for products and goods as well as services depends on who has access to this virtual liquidity.

What happened in Japan earlier, in 1997, is a general problem of our financial systems. Also, in the U.S., sixty per cent of commercial banks are much more restrictive in their policy to grant loans than the Federal Reserve estimates. This means that although the base rate is reduced by the Fed again and again, it is harder to get loans from banks and only at higher interest rates than ever before. Lending institutions justify such behavior by citing the slowing economy. This leads to many companies having difficulties to increase their liquidity to avoid collapses. The main problem in regard to the effects of interest policy is not that the base rate decides whether investments are made and jobs created, but who has access to liquidity and at which terms and conditions, and of course, who controls this access. Usually, this is governed by credit committees of the banks, but it is also controlled by the distribution mechanisms of the financial markets.

The later is less and less influenced by the central bank's interest policy.

For more than five years the United States was seen as the success model, accounting for an annual growth of nearly five per cent, decreasing unemployment, booming stock markets, price stability and even stunning budget surpluses. It appeared as if all economic goals were perfectly met. Clinton and Greenspan made possible what European governments were struggling with over the past decades. But was that really so? Yes, during the term of the two Clinton-administrations more than 8 million jobs were created, but without any health insurance, pension plans or Social Security. Millions of Americans have at least two, if not three, of these six-dollar-an-hour jobs, more than forty-one million Americans have no health insurance, while Social Security benefits were limited to a total of five years per capita, and limited to one time in a life. On the other hand, the number of inmates in U.S. federal or state prisons quadrupled since 1977. And since autumn, 2000, growth stagnated and major retailers employing over 38,000 people went bankrupt. Car dealers were sitting on new models, manufacturers like General Motors (15,000) and Daimler-Chrysler (26,000) reduced their work force significantly. Even a year before (1999), hundreds of thousands of jobs in the productive industries were cut, and even e-business and internet companies issued so-called "profit warnings," although these should rather be called losses. Stocks were falling. Dow Jones finished its worst year since 1981, losing 6.2 per cent in 2000. Nasdaq within one year lost 3000 billion U.S.-dollars. A sharp recession has followed despite Greenspan's attempts to fuel the economy by lowering the interest rate again and again. It's of no relevance for the financial markets if these figures represent only virtual economic potential, and are not linked in any way to real production of goods or services.

Important in this regard is the growing gulf between rich and poor in the United States. The differences have never been larger. Between 1977 and 1999 the net income of the richest one per cent of the society has risen by more than 115 per cent (clear of inflation), while the top 5 per cent of Americans could account for 43 per cent, and shocking for a rich nation like the United States, the net income of the bottom 5 per cent of society shrank by 9 per cent below the level of 1977. The middle class of three fifths of U.S. citizens were able to increase their purchasing power only a mere 8 per cent in twenty-two years, despite ten years of incredible boom.

A study of the Economic Policy Institute acknowledged "…that the gap between the pay of average U.S. workers and that of top corporate executives has exploded…" In 1980 it was a ratio of 42:1, but just before the 11 September attacks it was 419:1.[1]

This planet's real economic growth between 1980 and 2000 rose by 80 per cent, while the market capitalization at the world's stock markets generated a virtual growth of 1032 per cent during the same time. The Dow Jones alone, for instance, grew by an unreal 200 per cent between 1995 and 2000, some internet and new technology titles

---

1.   All figures from International Herald Tribune 6th September 1999

reached several thousands of percentage of growth, while the relationship between share prices and profit seems to be irrelevant. Stocks were
bought in order to sell these at a higher rate, and as long as everyone
believed in it the system worked. In 1996 Greenspan warned of an irra-
tionalism, which was only at its beginning.

The American boom of the nineties was largely created by the rise in
private consumption, but with real net income diverging as laid out
above, it was possible to finance such increased consumption only on
credit, consumer loans, credit cards, mortgages and personal loans
which led to the American people being indebted as they have never
been before. Private bankruptcy cases pile up in the courts, families are
destroyed, social existence becomes a privilege. On the other hand, it
isn't realistic to dream that the boom could have been initiated by
increased spending and consumption by the top 5 per cent of American society, as those very rich would not eat more, or buy more washing machines or many more cars than they already have. Middle class
Americans were not able to initiate this boom by their share (+8 per
cent consumer spending in twenty-two years) without financing or refinancing it by personal loans. So what justified the enormous virtual
growth reflected by the stock markets? Few real factors have to be taken
into consideration: There have been, of course, some significant
changes in the world after the collapse of the Communist regimes in
Eastern Europe and the Soviet Union. Opening of Eastern European
markets for the major internationals, access to resources and raw materials, privatisation, re-structuring, deregulation and industry-friendly
tax reforms in Western countries as well as in the emerging markets in
the former East generated a tremendous wealth in the western capitalistic countries. Whenever the U.S. economy was in danger of getting
stuck it was helped by an influx of cheap loans. And even stocks were
accepted as underlying security, although these "collaterals" were
heavily overvalued, but nevertheless served the only purpose: to buy
new and more overvalued shares. The Hausse fed itself. This mechanism was well alive in the nineties, since the volumen of loans of the

stock exchange-registered investment banks and stock traders trippled between 1994 and 1999, and reached unreal 278 billion dollars in March, 2000.

The trick employed by investment bankers was a simple one: refinanced by loans, the capital availbale for private but also institutional investors could operate with hedge funds and derivatives. This new liquidity, as virtual and principally unlimited as it was, fed the overheated stock market. This virtual and unreal financial bubble indeed had very real consequence on the actual and real economic cycles of production and consumption, and thus laid the ground for the American boom in the nineties.

This mechanism created an enormous wealth for the top 20 per cent of American society.

On the other side was an increasing indebtness, which also contributed to this boom, as it artificially and very short sightedly created a purchasing power that bounces back at the same pace rate at which the loans are called in by the banks. During the second half of the nineties, private debts of American households grew by 10 per cent annually and reached an unbelievable and very unhealthy 103 peer cent of the real income in 1999.

One need not be an economist to conclude that this could not go on for long. The IHT noted on 6 September, 1999, that "the gap between rich and poor in the U.S. widened to a record." This is the America Clinton and Gore formed. The FAZ [2] reported "The U.S. economy becomes vulnerable" as the performance deficit rose to 4.5 per cent of the GDP, commercial debt accounted for 63 per cent of the GDP (in 1994: 56 per cent), while loans taken out for purchasing stocks and shares amounted to 220 billion U.S. dollars in 1999, up from 126 billion USD in 1997. The total amount (nominal value) of stocks in the U.S. exploded in the Clinton-Gore years to an all time high of 170 per cent of the GDP, three times higher than the Activa of the banks. Forty-five per cent of the population had invested in stocks, even if

---

2.   Frankfurter Allgemeine Zeitung (FAZ) 22nd May 2000

they did it by borrowing, overborrowing and gambling with their pensions and retirement savings and homes.

According to the U.S. Department of Agriculture, more than 31 million Americans in 1999 were partly starving or at least had to worry about their next meal. More than 12 million children in the U.S. go to bed each night hungry. One of the first moves by the new Bush administration was not to attack this problem but to thank its supporters, the banks like MBNA America Bank, which donated 1.3 million U.S. dollars to Bush's campaign and demanded a change in the privat bankruptcy laws, which Clinton earlier had vetoed in Congress. Credit card companies could materialise their claims against highly indebted middle-class families who had been tempted by the aggressive marketing strategies of these credit card issuing banks but could not pay off their debts. Other beneficiaries of the new Bush government were those lobbying groups in Washington who were fighting for lowering standards in workers'-protection legislation. Bush already committed himself to a lifting of ergonomic standards, which means a backlash for any union fighting for those standards for many years. Other major Bush donors like the pharmaceutical industries achieved assurances that prices for their products won't be frozen, although the health care system would urgently require such a freeze.

And last but not least, the tax reform intends to lower the maximum income tax from 39.6 per cent to 35 per cent until 2006, while the lowest tax at 15 per cent remains unchanged, meaning that for three quarters of the American population nothing changed at all. At the same time, the inheritance allowance would be raised from 675,000 U.S. dollars to 3.5 million U.S. dollars, all this in a time the U.S. had to deal with a threat of a depression as serious than the great depression before the Second World War. In October, 2001, more than 700,000 Americans lost their jobs, sending the unemployment rate into orbit (within a month from 4.9% per cent to 5.4 per cent;, in 2000 it was still at 3.9 per cent) hitting 7 per cent in spring, 2002. In the year 2001 alone more than two million lost their jobs, and by this their social existence as in the U.S. unemployment compensation is paid only for six months and covers only 50 per cent of the previous salary. Meanwhile, economic growth shrank by 0.4 per cent[3]. Although the U.S. economy was in recession, Americans consumed as never before. The performance deficit rose from 4 per cent of the GDP up to 6 per cent. In order to finance this deficit the U.S. needed an influx of 2 billion U.S. dollars foreign investment per day. As this is highly unlikely, the devaluation of the dollar is inevitable. Until recently (2000) the deficit financing has been conducted by foreign direct investments and by selling stocks. Nowadays, 95 per cent are financed through bonds, which are much more expensive. Because the interest on those bonds are relatively high, America will have more and more difficulties paying off its debt. According to Handelsblatt,[4] there would be only two options: either the dollar will devalue radically by at least 43 per cent, thus making American products incredibly cheap and trigger an export boom, or the foreign demand for U.S. products had to rise by 23 per cent if the dollar rebounded.

At present, many American economists and analysts fear that the U.S. could experience the same malaise as Japan, which has not recovered since the bubble of financial and real estate markets burst at the end of the eighties. The collaps of the stock market in the U.S. led to a loss of 4,500 billion U.S. dollars in assets for U.S. investors.[5] Because of highly exaggerated profit expectations, many companies are highly indebted now, as they expanded tremendously and created over-capacities. Only two facts have so far prevented the worst: low interest rates enabled regular citizens to re-finance their loans and mortgages and consume the money they saved, and secondly, the rise in the real estate sector allowed them to access higher mortgages on their homes. Both effects are quite limited and can not be expanded indefinetly.

---

3.   Handelsblatt 4th January 2002
4.   Handelsblatt 22nd February 2002
5.   Handelsblatt 15th July 2002

The average American today is indebted by more than 105 per cent of his annual income. Fifteen per cent of incomes are usually spent on interest and repayment of principal. With stocks falling, more than 80 million Americans lost 2000 billion dollars within weeks. A person who two years earlier invested 10,000 U.S. dollars in diversified stock funds only had 2,200 U.S. dollars in his portfolio in 2002. The overall economic data before 11th September, 2001, showed dramatic slow-downs: GNP shrank at pace rate, growth figures for 2001, previously expected to be 1.2 per cent, reached only 0.3 per cent. The trade balance also turned neagtive. In August, 2002, the trade deficit was 38,46 billion U.S. dollars, exports dropped by another 1.3 per cent, while imports steadily rose by 2 per cent.[6]

The double deficit of the Reagan years led to devaluation of the dollar. The triple deficit (budget, performance and trade deficits) of today will lead to depression, especially since the U.S. dollar is now rivaled by the EURO. The U.S. is missing a 400-billion-dollar-influx of foreign capital annually if its leaders want to compensate the performance deficit of 6,5 per cent of the GNP, to which it will climb by the end of this year (2003). Under these circumstances war appears to be the only way out.

The collapse of the American economy was predictable, and the events of 11th September, 2001, only accelerated the decline and in a way rescued the president-in-charge who gave a weak performance until he could declare a war, a war which NASDAQ did not want, as the shares were dwindling even faster. Dow Jones instead needed such a war, and the stocks of heavy industry, manufacturers and especially the oil industry grew at rapid pace. This planet has to be grateful to NASDAQ that only a war and not a major world war loomed from the oil industry's lobbyists (more than thirty senior Bush administration officials) hunger for retaliation.

It is probably due to the influence of NASDAQ industries that we are still alive, as the cowboy and former business partner of Bin Laden

---

6.   Handelsblatt 21st October 2002

would not have hesitated a split second if he could have launched a major war, with all the consequences we Europeans were able to foresee.

2. An American Coup

What the events of 11th September 2001 really were and whether this was a state-organised crime or a right-wing coup will remain unclear unless one analyzes what has happend in the wake of it. It has been clear for a while that something had to happen if the economic disaster of the two Clinton and half a year of Bush administrations had to be covered up. The world was not facing an economic slowdown because of the American economic misbehaviour, not a recession, nothing else than a depression as dangerous as in 1929. It was also clear that American imperialism would not just collapse or implode without taking others with them. Imperialists, like ordinary capitalists, don't like to hear it but they behave like butchers in a slaughterhouse, if only they can get some of their valuables in a safe place and survive. Whoever stands in their way has to fall. They simply don't see that in the end they are the only ones left who then stand in the door, in their own way, so to say. Even states are not safe from those psychopaths who control most of our world economically and thereby politically.

In this sense it might have been a good idea for the Schröder-Fischer gang to declare their "unlimited solidarity" with the United States, as not doing so immediately would have meant being seen as a potential enemy, especially when some of the suspects had links to or were coming from Germany.

But there is a difference between declaring solidarity and responding to demands for military support, which clearly have not been made by the United States.[7]

In addition to the much-too-early-declared unlimited solidarity with the United States, Schröder had another problem: even if the

---

7. International Herald Tribune 7th November 2001

story of the single maniac Bin Laden and his Al Qaida fighters was true, there was not only no hard evidence for such accusations which could be held up in any court,[8] but questions regarding why secret services, which had some degree of knowledge about the planned attacks, did not come forward, or why and by whom they were silenced. The Frankfurter Allgemeine Zeitung on 12th September, 2001, published an article in which secret services claim that for more than six months they had hints of the planned attacks. And a former MI6 agent is quoted as saying that a major reorganisation would be required, and that it is absolutely unbelievable that those organizations had not been undermined or at least infiltrated.[9]

Der Spiegel even went further in claiming that western secret services had knowdledge of the plans of Bin Laden to use hijacked planes to target the World Trade Center, Sears Tower and the CIA headquarter in Langley as early as 1995.[10]

So it can not be seen as a complete surprise, although most of the secret services might not have known the exact day and time it was going to happen. It may make us suspicious that it happend *before* the start of the business day, and one should ask why it did not happen two hours later, as the effect would have been much more worse. Unthinkable, but the number of victims may well have been in the region of 30,000 instead of the 3,000, and even if one should not see any difference in the functions human beings are carrying out, whether they are cleaning personnel or top managers, from the point of view of these evil attackers the difference in the effect their deeds might have had would be significant. Who convinced the terrorists not to attack between 11 and noon? Has there been a secret agenda? Isn't it rather strange that the U.S. administration seemed to be unaware of the existence of a group able to carry out the 11th September attacks, but after those occurred was immediately able to present bin Laden and his ter-

---

8.   Financial Times 5th October 2001
9.   Frankfurter Allgemeine Zeitung 12th September 2001
10.   SPIEGEL Online 7th December 2001

ror network "Al Quaida"? It is even more striking that the high ranking New York Times editor, William Safire, asserted that the terrorists at least must have had access to information in several of the twenty-six secret services in the U.S. Who were the contacting persons? Why didn't they come forward? Did they 'only' let "it" happen, or did they even give instructions? Why did the CIA meet with bin Laden in Dubai in July, 2001, just weeks before the attacks, as the French paper "Le Figaro" writes? Did they only bring flowers for Osama, who was hospitalised for his kidney dysfunction?

Why isn't it investigated thoroughly that the alledged hijackers, even after almost 600 training hours, weren't able to steer a plane, not even a Cessna, and that according to the flying school, one of the two was too stupid to even drive a car, as the Miami Herald and other newspapers in Florida write? Why didn't the pilots press the May-day buttons when they realized that they were hijacked? (Maybe they weren't.) And why did one of the main suspects, Atta, use a flight from Portland, Oregon, which if it had been delayed only by a few minutes would not have allowed him to make it to his connecting flight, the one that crashed into the first tower? Would a terrorist really risk missing his most important and last flight ever? How come, despite a supposedly perfect system to protect U.S. territory against Soviet missiles, did the second and third planes cruise around for more than an hour after the first attack? Why should the suspects check in with their clear names, pay for the tickets by their own credit cards, etc.? I spoke with a Swissair captain, who said it would be very unlikely that someone with limited knowledge about flying would be able to steer a plane in a military style attack into a building. He also said that if someone tried to kill him in his seat the aircraft would probably dive, and if someone were threatening to kill him if he did not fly into a building, he, as every other pilot of moral integrity, would rather try to crash the plane in the harbor if he had no other option and knew that he would not survive. Since 11th September, 2001, all airport authorities around the world pretend to fight terrorism by confiscating cosmetic sizzors and other "dangerous devices" from passengers. We will soon be told that long fingernails can be used as a weapon and many of us will have long fingernails once all scissors have been confiscated. The U.S. wants the world to believe the most unlikely story about 11th September, 2001, and only a few dare to ask whether the official version makes sense. Who has really been behind the attacks? How come the victims in the rubble could in many cases be identified by their teeth, if the official version tells us that the black box could not be found and the voice recorders be heard?

It may be evil and unpatriotic to ask those questions, but as journalists we have to ask any question.

There are no reasonable answers, unless one asks who benefitted from the attacks, and this can be answered clearly: some of the major oil and energy industries of the United States of America.

And, of course, a sitting president, who got into the White House only by a bitterly contested election, mocking any democratic principles the U.S. constitution promotes.

3. Terrorism is when one throws bombs but has no army for that...

In 1996, the government of Sudan made an offer to Bill Clinton that it would extradite Bin Laden, but the U.S. rejected that offer.[11] Why? The U.S. administration advised Sudan to expel Bin Laden, who went to the only other country where he would be accepted, Afghanistan.

It can also not be seen as a complete surprise that Afghanistan was chosen, as the U.S. has sent weapons worth 3 billion dollars every year since 1980 to the Mujaheddin in Kabul, laying the ground for resistance against the Soviets. At least this is the official version. And even former CIA director Robert Gates writes in his memoirs "From the Shadows" that American secret services had supported the Mujahedin as early as six months before the Soviet invasion. Asked whether he

---

11.   Berliner Zeitung 26th October 2001)

would confirm this, former security adviser Brzezinski said "Yes, officially we always maintained that CIA supported the Mujahedin during 1980, well after the intervention of the Soviets, which started on 24th December, 1979, but in reality, President Carter issued the first directive for inofficial CIA support for the opposition against the pro-Soviet regime in Kabul on 3rd July, 1979. And on the same day I wrote a note for the president in which I warned that this might trigger an intervention by the Soviets." [12]

Brzezinski also admits later in the same interview that American support for the Mujahedin led to an increase in Islamic fundamentalist activities, which he justifies, as this undermined the Soviet system, even brought it down and freed Eastern Europe while ending the cold war peacefully, he says.

It does not sound too far fetched if one blames U.S. strategy itself for indirectly provoking the events of 11th September, 2001.

It is interesting in this regard that the U.S. failed to present the evidence they claimed they were holding against the terror group of Bin Laden. The Financial Times asserted on 5th October, 2001, that "the document appeared more calculated to persuade the public of the merits of military action in Afghanistan." And the same article went on: "…The document also provides only a partial account of Mr. bin Ladn's background, and makes no mention of how the U.S. agencies supported Mr. bin Laden when he fought against the former Soviet Union's occupation of Afghanistan. The document mentions financial holding companies like "Laden International" and "Taba Investments". Tony Blair's spokesman admitted the "document did not provide a case against Mr. Bin Laden that would stand up in a court of law." So, if the secret services had no knowledge of the 'devil's' investments, how come that he could run companies bearing his own name or the name of his group? And if "evidence" presented would not stand up in a court of law, well, can it then be justification for a legal military

---

12.   Interview with Brzezinski in French weekly Le Nouvel Observateur, 15-21 January 1998

action if there is something like that (it sounds like a contradiction of itself, but that's the terminology of our system) of which many thousands if not millions in the end fall victim? Is it really only "Wild West" ideology that makes them shoot first and then ask? Is that civilized?

"Evidence from U.S. points to bin Laden", writes the Financial Times on 5th October, 2001, but the newspaper also reported, "…diplomats said they did not doubt at all that the attack had come from abroad. But they added that the U.S. presentation could not show, beyond doubt, real factual, hard evidence, apart from the names of several of the hijackers, details where those hijackers had studied and their backgrounds." This describes very well the problems the U.S. and British governments had in gathering public support for their military actions. Although public support was weak in European nations, their leaders were intriguing against each other as during Bismarck's time. Of course, all this happend behind closed doors, but soon one could read in the New York Times[13] that the "Northern Alliance no longer opposes foreign peace keeping force…but would prefer if the international forces came from Islamic countries." And certainly not from the U.S. or Great Britain, which have already made their preparations. Britain especially was eager to lead the force.

The German Frankfurter Allgemeine Zeitung on the same day[14] instead offered a contradicting version. Quoting the special envoy for Afghanistan to the UN, Brahimi, that a European country that has no burdens in its past concerning Afghanistan would be the only acceptable solution. And, of course, the FAZ goes on to stake the claim for the Germans by advocating that only Spain and Germany would fulfill this criteria. And if that were not enough, the FAZ accused the British government of putting considerable pressure on Afghani parties to accept the "peacekeeping" force led by them.

---

13.   International Herald Tribune 30th November 2001
14.   Frankfurter Allgemeine Zeitung 30th November 2001

Funny that the same German newspaper seems to have no problem advocating German participation in the wars against Yugoslavia, and later the German leadership in the Kosovo "peace-keeping" mission, although German troops in a country that has already suffered two times before under German military occupation will fear the third time in less than 100 years. That, of course, is German hypocrisy.

4. Has it really been such a surprise?

On 17th May, 2002, the International Herald Tribune (IHT) headlined "Parties press Bush on Sept. 11 warning", laying bare that there was at least a failure of intelligence, but it also suggests that the White House ignored warnings on 15th August, 2001. "Not just Democrats but some Republicans expressed concern about the report, confirmed by the White House, that Bush had been told in a daily CIA intelligence briefing at his Texas ranch in early August, that terrorists linked to Osama bin Laden were seeking to hijack aircraft," writes Brian Knowlton in the IHT. "There was a lot of information,' Senator Richard Shelby of Alabama, a senior Republican and vice chairman of the Senate Intelligence Committee, said Thursday on NBC-TV. If it had been acted upon properly, we may have had a different situation on September 11." And while the warnings separately lacked detail of the September 11 plot, Shelby said: "You tie them together with other warnings, and I believe you have a lot to work on"[15]

Well, who has an interest in dismantling the president, when to criticize him had been seen as unpatriotic? Despite the fact that mid-term elections were near, and even some potential candidates for the 2004 presidential contest might have thought they could feed their apsirations, the fact that Senator Shelby is not only an expert in secret services, and as one of the chairpersons in the committee has access to a lot of classified information, but is also a member of the same party as Bush, denounces speculation that the mid-term elections or any profli-

---

15. International Herald Tribune 17th May 2002

gacy of single senators have anything to do with the sudden revelations. So what makes conservative papers like the Washington Post and TV networks like NBC and CNN cross-examine the president's knowledge in a way that may make him appear as a weak leader, even a suspect in a conspiracy to let things happen in order to be able to counter-strike? Of course, as we can read in papers like the Guardian, or on 18th May, 2002, in the IHT, it had been planned some considerable time before the 'attack' to move against bin Laden and the network previously financed by CIA and other U.S. branches.

While the president's own security adviser, Condolezza Rice, former high-ranking official at oil producer Chevron, was quick to defend her boss by saying that the CIA memo of August was only one and a half pages long and therefore not detailed enough to grasp a clear warning from it, one could burst into laughter, since the president himself, as a candidate in the 2000 campaign, said that he would not pay any attention to documents exceeding one or two pages and could not concentrate in meetings for more than thirty minutes. On the other hand, the Genova G 7 summit of May, 2001, experienced an increased security as the U.S. suggested that the Italian prime minister order anti-aircraft missiles be stationed around the summit facilities, as terrorists theoretically could threaten to use hijacked aircraft as missiles. So if they knew it in May, why be surprised to read in a CIA memo in August that such a thing could happen in the near future?

In fact, the Senate committee investigating events prior to September 11 found in a report being pubished on 28th August, 2002,[16] that "a veritable blueprint" for the events known under September 11, had been known by various secret services, which the report cites as having failed terribly. Well, this sounds like a fairy tale. Secret Services may fail, but usually they don't. They can for obvious reasons not advertise their successes. Nor can they contradict sufficiently if someone criti-

---

16. IHT/New York Times 28th &29th August 2002/DER SPIEGEL 19th September 2002

cises them. The truth is, secret services don't fail to such an extent unless they are told to.

It is certainly not owed to a free press and eager journalism alone that these facts are presented just less than a year after the most patriotic and unifying moment of U.S. history since World War II, as these facts have been spread around by other journalists, most of them abroad for a while, but one always liked to let them appear as conspiracy theories although, I must say, what would be wrong with that? I have not seen any party, political group, historical event, any form of living together of even small groups of people or societies without conspiracy. It happens to be everywhere, so why not have theories for it as well, especially if these provide more logical answers than the published 'truth' or official versions. After all, these facts are designed to discredit the president who lost the election and was brought to power in a coup-like maneuver by—let's put it bluntly—the oil industry and some white collar criminals he later defied, as the ENRON and World-Com scandals broke, and when he had to distance himself from them wouldn't he want to risk being seen in the same light. The truth is that a president and vice president, who would be serving prison sentences today if the rules they introduced in the wake of the scandals had been in effect ten years ago, have no moral power anymore. The question indeed is whether an administration that won the bitterly contested election only in the courtrooms ever had any moral impetus.

It also fits too perfectly into the general anti-Islamic mood when TV showed celebrating Muslims who seemed to be dancing because of the September 11 attacks. The German ARD TV report *Panorama* proved on 20th September, 2001, that these footages were fakes. Dancing Palestinians were asked by U.S. camera teams to celebrate, and even got chocolate cookies for this as the German camera team filmed. The idea was to make the western world hostile to Muslims and create a climate of mistrust and hostility. This was laying the ground for the anthrax phobia that U.S. media and secret services wanted to link to Islamic terrorists or even Saddam Hussein, but again they failed. The rest of the world simply didn't buy their lies.[17]

One could read that the FBI assumed that right-wing extremists in the U.S. were trying to fool around. All letters containing anthrax spores had the same origin and were produced or multiplied in a U.S. laboratory, selling it off to other laboratories in the U.S. Anthrax cultures stemming from the Soviet Union or Iraq (if they had any) carry completely different marks. Moreover, a long time before the September 11-events, the FBI investigated right-wing and facist groups in connection with threats by them to use anthrax, which they also sent a few times. One almost forgot about the Oklahoma City building attack, which was carried out by exactly one of these fascist gangs, the so called "Aryan Action Group". No one asks why this terrorist gang, which in part is playing into the hands of the industrial military complex of the U.S., has not been blamed with the attacks of 11th September? It would have been at least one possibility. But of course, the Bush administration had something different in mind. In order to be able to launch a "counter-attack," they would need for the enemy to come from outside the U.S., and not from within it. Therefore, one can assume that Uncle Sam was and is blind in his right eye.

What happened in the wake of the first military successes was the greatest human rights violation of the past decades of U.S. history. Even the IHT states on 30th November that "few detained in U.S. sweep are linked to terrorism," and that of the "1200 detained after September 11, 603 are still held, most of them not linked to any terrorism but visa and immigration law violations. Only ten or eleven are believed to have any relationship to the terrorist group al Quaida."[18] Is this the new America? Bush, Cheney, Rice, Ashcroft are reforming the country in a way that has not been done since the McCarthy years. It is difficult to say where they take their moral impetus from when criticizing Russia, China, North Korea and Iraq. A country that disregards

---

17.   LVZ 24th October 2001
18.   International Herald Tribune 30th November 2002

international treaties, conventions, human rights and civilized standards while terrifying the rest of the world by its nuclear and biological
weapons is considered a *rogue state*, unless it is the United States itself,
or Israel, which, as the BBC stated on 24th May, 2003, is probably one
of the countries in the Middle East that has a vast arsenal of undeclared
chemical and biological weapons and a secret nuclear weapon program.

In this aspect it is important to draw attention to the victims of the
U.S. economic downturn in the aftermath of 11th September. These
victims are mainly to be found in the so-called "Third World". And
even if the September attacks had not happend, the economic downturn, or slowdown as the Bush administration first called it while it was
already a recession and soon will turn out to be a depression of the kind
like in 1929, was imminent, and if not for the events in September it
would have led to the same cruel consequences for the poorest of our
planet.

"Vast Global Toll Forecast from the Sept. 11 Attacks," headlines the
IHT.[19]And it goes on: "…As many as 40,000 children under the age of
five will die, and some 10 million more will be condemned to poverty
because of the terrorist attacks in the United States on Sept. 11, the
president of the World Bank said Sunday. Mr. Wolfenson said the economic fallout from the attacks would cause several poor countries to
stall or fall into recession…there is an absolutely clear link between the
drop in economic activity and infant mortality and poverty". The only
point in which Wolfenson is wrong is in saying that this is related only
to the September 11-attacks. This would have happend anyhow; that is
how our system is structured. And it is also owed to our so-called "free
press" in a so-called "western democracy," which always pretends to
defend freedom of speech and the cause of human rights, that this
media does not put an effort into publishing this fact, as it would necessarily lead to certain questions which would fundamentally change
our economic system if mankind really took human rights and free-

---

19. (IHT 01 Oct. 2001)

dom seriously. The 3000 victims in the World Trade Center are not the only ones who are innocent.

5. Reaganomics was superior to Clintonmania but couldn't compete with it...

Late President Ronald Reagan has always been portrayed by both, his followers as well as his opponents as someone who fought vigorously for a free market and lower taxes. The opposite is probably true. The US market under President Reagan had more trade barriers than any time in the history of the country and once the Reagan administration realized that the lower income taxes introduced emptied the pockets of the state which had to deal with a triple deficit (trade, budget & performance) they reversed and increased taxes again. It also fell under the Reagan presidency that a social security fund had been created and fed by taxes steeming from higher income taxes. In fact, it has been President Clinton who lowered taxes drastically. This lead to the consequences we saw in the wake of 11th September 2001. And it was also Clinton who cut on social expenditure introducing legislation which limits the time span of social security benefits to five years per person and life. The myth, of course, is the other way around. Reagan always wanted to appear less socialistic than he was, Clinton less capitalistic than he was. One associates Reagan with a tax policy feeding the rich and being cruel in his social policy while Clinton enjoys to have the image of having been a more socialistic and liberal president. Clinton's tax cuts fed the virtual reality casinos of NASDAQ and DOW JONES and it has been Bush who pledged to further cut taxes citing the necessity to employ Reagonomics to bring the economy back on track. It sounds like a joke that Bush JR seems to have not even any knowledge about what his dad and President Reagan did during their presidencies. Nevertheless, he has to deal with a triple deficit as well nowadays. The US' budget for 2005 has increased by 3.5% to 2,400 billion Dollars of which the biggest share goes to the military sector (+7.1%) amounting unprecedented 400 billion Dollars, while the budget for the so called "Homeland Security" agenda accounts for the third largest share, having increased by 9.7% to 30 billion Dollars. Healthcare, still the second largest share in the budget will be reduced by 1.6% to 68 billion Dollars. All this will be financed by new debts which will amount to 4.5% of the GNP or 521 billion Dollars. Under present conditions the US would not qualify for participation in the Euro. Not that I see them ever be led into temptation to join the Frankfurt-Club but it is a funny thought that the US who always claims that they are managing the world currency markets and provide stability would not meet the strict criteria set forth in the Maastricht accord of the EU. Financing nothing else but their military adventures which until today seem not to be able to generate a good return on investment lets their currency become weaker and weaker. The only economic recovery seen in the US now is in the military industrial and airlines complex. All other business decline or stagnate. The Financial Times has been worrying about the "slowdown in household expenditure" which seems to be more persistent than the FED suggests.[20] "It is not unusual for economic growth to be uneven from month to month during periods of economic expansions and whereas Socialism tries to protect against crisises Capitalism takes advantage of those. But the combination of slower than expected growth in the second quarter (of 2004), high energy prices and a weak labour market has once again raised questions about the durability of the US recovery", writes Andrew Balls in the FT. It appears that the businesses have focused on reducing costs rather than increasing investment. The growth the Bush White House wants voters to believe in is a fake as it only happens by cutting down jobs and by this increasing profit margins which will be very short-lived. The weak domestic demand in the US will further decline as consumers can only spend what they got in their pockets and those who are not on the payroll won't be able to increase spending but will be forced to cut down. And the Bush-junta's increased budgets for the military

20. Financial Times 18th August 2004

complex won't encourage consumers at all as the ordinary American household won't buy a cruise missile or patriot rocket unless CNN convinces them that this is the only way to protect themselves against Bin Ladn.

6. US-system offers political choice but no alternative……

The Americans under Bush may realize that their system offers a political choice but no political alternative as Kerry in most policy issues does not explicitly differ from the White House strategy as he would not withdraw troops from Afghanistan and Iraq and would certainly also not change the fiscal and economical agenda fundamentally. Kerry always expected to be taken serious, Bush has to be taken serious. About Kerry noone makes jokes, about Bush one can not laugh. The US Democrats must have been told by someone that they better don't try to win the 2004 elections otherwise they had nominated Senator Rodham-Clinton right away. She is probably even more dangerous than her husband was as she really seems to be bright and exactly this could be the reason for parts of the military-industrial complex to mistrust her. What if they want the president to attack a country and lets say she was president and ask why? There wouldn't be a sex scandal at hand to make pressure on her like it was common practice with her husband. Once he rejected demands to bomb the Iraqi no-fly zone a scandal unfolded and a few days later he did bomb innocent people. No, Mrs Rodham-Clinton would not offer a political choice but an alternative and that's why she was told not to run this time. Four years down the road, one may need someone like her to put things right again. After eight desastrous war years with Bush, even the US will need to take breath for a moment and why not have a well-respected lady push through another neoliberal agenda with an ice-cold smile which will serve her credibility as she always appeared to be able to control herself better than her husband.

7. U.S.-Russian rivalry

There has been some reluctance to the U.S. attacks in Afghanistan in the Arab world as well.

Just two weeks before the coup attempt of September 11 in the U.S. the Financial Times reported that Azerbaijan's President Heydar Aliyev criticised Iran for militarizing the Caspian Sea, using gunboats to stake its claim to oil exploration blocs. However, BP was said to lead the consortium that had been awarded the right by Azerbijan "to develop the concession, known as Alov to the Azeris and Alborz to Iranians...Coinciding with the Iranian's visit was the arrival in Baku of Elizabeth Jones, U.S. assistant secretary of state. U.S. oil companies such as ExxonMobil and Chevron are heavily involved in offshore exploration in the Azeri sector.[21]

All this speaks for the "conspiracy theory," as there had been no other interest in the region from the very beginning. A few weeks after this incident it became possible to solve all military problems by laying bomb carpets in retaliation of what is yet not fully established, and although there is legitimate doubt whether the attacks against the World Trade Center and Pentagon really came from abroad, and if so how much was known or even provoked by U.S. and other secret services. No matter what, the fact that the war in Afghanistan was not the "war against terrorism" the U.S. administration wants the American people and the rest of the world to believe, but a war over geo-strategic predominance and resources. And one may call it colonial, as the findings are significant and will justify military presence for the exploiting nations for many years, as a survey published in the FT on 11th December, 2000, claims that the oil and gas finds near Kazakstan may be bigger than the North Sea. Even before the September 11-events the U.S. re-established a stringent energy program which had been employed during the oil crisis in 1973-74. The Berliner Zeitung reported on 6th June 2001, that the U.S. had discovered a new interest

---

21. Fiancial Times (FT) 30th August 2001

in the Caspian region as the conflict in the Middle East as well as the energy crisis in California provoked by privatizations made it appear necessary to explore such possibilities. This is, of course, only partly correct, as the Clinton administration already followed the oil industry's demand and established strategic ties with the former Soviet Union republics nearby.[22]

Especially the then vice president and later presidential candidate Al Gore was involved in such negotiations, but the oil industry probably did not trust him to be able to trigger the war they regarded as necessary in order to "protect American interests abroad". A high ranking Pentagon official, David Trucker, said in an interview on 16th October, 2001, that "there is only one region which for the U.S. is worth fighting for. It is the region from the Persian Gulf to the Caspian Sea and Central Asia, as 75 per cent of the world's oil reserves are to be found there, while there are 33 per cent of the gas reserves".[23]

And the liberal German weekly Die Woche wrote on 19th October, 2001, that "a blessed shower of petro-dollars was raining down on the presidential candidates, while George W. Bush received more than 80 per cent of the campaign contributions made by the oil industry." It is obvious that the donors expected something in return, something which ultimately materialised when the campaign against Afghanistan was launched right after the "unforeseen" terrorist attacks from 11th September, 2001. We speak of Enron, Exxon, BP, Chevron, Texaco who even supported the transition from Clinton to Bush by a high-ranking team of oil industry managers, of which more than twenty were on the board of the Bush team when conquering the White House after the coup-like Florida election controversy. A survey carried out by the private organization Judicial Watch screening all donations to the Bush campaign in 2000 exceeding 500,000 Dollars proves that those donations very well paid-off after Iraq had been attacked. For one donated Dollar a "return on investment" of 20 Dollars has been

---

22.   International Herald Tribune 19th November 1999).
23.   Tageszeitung (TAZ) 16th October 2001

materialized until today. The donors clearly profitted from Bush's military adventures. The former CEO of Enron, Kenneth Lay, who had several business projects in the central Caucasian region, fought vigorously for the "new" energy concept in which Vice President Cheney proclaimed the return to fossil energy and deregulation of the oil industry. Security adviser Condolezza Rice has been a member of the board of Chevron, and both Bush and Cheney earned their money in the Texan oil business. Just a second before his nomination as vice president, Cheney arranged a major oil deal between Haliburton Corp. and Azerbaijan. Just hours after the start of the war against Afghanistan, the Chevron-Texaco stocks climed up to 93.45 U.S. dollars. Even more interesting is the fact that Osama bin Laden and President-in-charge George W. Bush know each other as business partners from the eighties and early nineties when Osama bin Ladens brother in law, Khalid ibn Mahfouz, former member of the board of directors of the BCCI (Bank for Credit and Commerce International), which was closed down because of allegations of money laundering for drug cartells in 1987) bought stocks worth a billion U.S. dollars, thus owning 11.5 per cent of the oil company Harken, which between 1986 and 1993 was led by George W Bush. [24]

Especially old Bush, who at least was an elected president of his country, is using the Carlyle Group, an international investment fund, to work for the Saudi family of bin Laden. "The idea that the father of the president, himself a former president, is doing business with a company being investigated by the FBI for its alledged involvement in the terror attacks on September 11, is terrifying," writes the U.S. magazine 'Judicial Watch'. But there must have been more insiders, especially in financial circles at Wall Street.

During the week before the attacks, trade in stocks which should have plunged in the aftermath of September 11, rose by 1200 per cent. These stocks were sold very expensively before the attack, but were

---

24. James Woolsey, former CIA Director quoted in Jean Charles Brisard's "The Forbidden Truth"

bound to be transferred some time later. Thus the vendors were able to buy the same stocks at the same rate after the crash and make tremendous profits. The stocks from the two airlines were involved, but also those of major financial players like Morgan Stanley and Merryll-Lynch, who occupied some twenty-two floors in the World Trade Center. Moreover, these insiders, whoever they were and whereever they obtained their informations from, bought U.S. treasury bonds worth 5 billion U.S. dollars in expectation that after the attacks those would rise significantly. Why didn't the U.S. government launch an investigation into these financial circumstances? The Security and Exchange Commission usually is eager to investigate any major speculation which can not be explained by reasonable means. Unless those questions are fully answered the speculations will feed conspiracy theories about the U.S. administration's personal knowledge and possible involvement, especially since it becomes more and more obvious, so that a source like the British paper Guardian reported that the war against Afghanistan was planned by the Bush administration right from the beginning and before the events of 11th September, 2001.

And the German weekly magazine Wirtschaftswoche [25]puts it bluntly, citing "legitimate interests" of the U.S. oil industry, to which Afghanistan has always been of special interests: "Fight against terrorism also requires securing the supply with oil. In 1997 Marty Miller, vice president of the American Unocal group, negotiated with the Taliban about laying a pipeline from Turkmenistan through Afghanistan to the Pakistani coast." Also, the IHT writes under the headline, "Chevron Texaco merger reflects oil's new face,"[26] that some of the "largest new oil fields in the world have been discovered far from the Middle East, mainly in the deep waters off Brazil and West Africa and the Caspian Sea...now takes on new polictical and technical perils, from the spasmodic civil war in Angola to the depths of the Caspian..." That explains why the oil lady, Condolezza Rice, who was one

---

25. Wirtschaftswoche, 4th October 2001
26. International Herald Tribune 17th October 2000

of the managers of the Chevron-Texaco merger, became "security" adviser in the Bush-Cheney White House. The pipelines in the Caspian region and securing the permanent influence in the gulf region became top policy priorities in the U.S. administration.

This venture, of course, was designed to become less dependent on OPEC while making use of the oil fields in the Caspian region which were easily accessible after the Soviet Union collapsed in 1991. According to Wirtschaftswoche, the initial approach of the Clinton administration was to lay a pipeline from Turkmenistan via Azerbaijan, Georgia to Turkey, but this would be politically somewhat delicate, as it would cross traditionally unsafe Kurdish territorry in Turkey. However, this would have been the only realistic alternative to the route via Afghanistan, while sidelining Iran and Russia, writes Witschaftswoche.

And it also observed some kind of reluctance of the Bush administration to support the route accross turkish Kurdistan, as this would strengthen the Kurdish movement and undermine the authority of the best ally of the U.S. in the region. However, on 19th September, 2002, BBC reported that the agreement on this pipeline route had been executed. The main interest still would, of course, be the Afghanistan route for which arrangements had been made a while before. While the Clinton administration was eager to sideline the Russian Federation, Bush and his people seem to accept that they had better cooperate with President Putin and let them participate. They also just recently helped the Russians to develop pipelines to Murmansk, a historic place of U.S. weapon support during the Second World War, and one now speaks of the Russians supplying the U.S. with oil through Murmansk and securing the lifeline should the next major war interrupt oil supply from the gulf region. On 30th November, 2001, the IHT reported under the headline "In Russia, U.S. Sees a Rising Oil Giant," that a major development was the 2.6-billion-dollar pipeline built by a Chevron Texaco consortium (Condolezza Rice was member of the board) "...from oil fields in Kazakhstan to the Russian port of Novorossisyks on the Black Sea.

Knowing this helps to understand why Russian armed forces as well as the Federal Security Service want to make sure that Chechnya remains under Russian domination and control, especially since it "...has minor oil reserves and is near the pipeline route from the Caspian Sea region to the Black Sea."[27]

According to this article, Khattab, a Jordanian fighter in Chechnya, over the years "received funds from Afghanistan as well as Muslim charities in oil-rich states. The Muslim group makes up at least 60 per cent of the full-time guerilla forces in Chechnya, a western diplomat said." So some of the money the Americans send to Afghanistan was probably used by those Chechnyan terrorists who later forced the world to hold its breath when keeping 900 people hostage in a Moscow theatre, a move which let the Russians agree to the Pax Americana in the Security Council when it came to Iraq. The Americans wanted to attack Iraq, but the Russians opposed their unfulfillable UN draft resolutions in the Security Council. Now that the Russians had (American-financed) terrorism in their own capital, it would allow them to crack down on Chechnya. The U.S. probably offered to abstain from any criticism over Chechny if Russia in exchange would not criticize the U.S. for its Iraq venture.

The only difference was that Russia had to defend itself on its own territorry and had to keep the country together, while America simply wanted to attack a foreign and sovereign country. One would not be taken by wonder if the U.S. had another terrorist attack at home as well, maybe just around the November, 2004, election since the September 11-events didn't keep its momentum, and more and more Americans withdrew their support for the actions condoned by the Bush-Cheney-Rice-Ashcroft administration. In the end, these new attacks would be linked to Al Quaida and Bin Laden. In this scenario one would not be surprised if Bin Laden and his fighters were found playing with a nuclear ignition device. Then, we who criticize the U.S. for its imperialism would be proven wrong.

---

27.   International Herald Tribune 19th November 2001

8. Russian-EU-strategic partnership

Whereas the U.S. and Russia are rivals—again or still—the German approach is very different. Since the Germans gave up their plans to participate in the oil ventures of the U.S. and UK, as they would only be in the back seat and have been left in Kosovo, which gives them some trouble since they lead the "peacekeeping" forces there as well as in Afghanistan, where they lead the UN forces together with the Netherlands, while the Americans and British build up their bases which the UN forces can't make use of and are somewhat sidelined, the German energy industry decided to concentrate on their elaborate relationship with the Russian gas sector. Especially after the GAZPROM privatization and selling off to the West, mainly Germany, in exchange for NATO expansion, agreed to under Yeltsin, Germany had more than a foot in the door. But why is it that Russia makes such unfavorable deals?

It may have something to do with the Russian situation itself. Life expectancy for men dropped significantly from seventy-three to fifty-eight years since the Soviet Union was dissolved, as Tony Benn, Labor MP, said in an interview.[28] The "Red Ben" in that interview went on saying that the last thing those new NATO members with all their economic difficulties needed were weapons. "We lend them money and they buy weapons from us, then we exploit their markets and force them to cut down on social spending," Benn says.

Whether one agrees with this Labor MP, who is known for decades for his leftist views, or not, the facts he presents are undoubtable. First of all, there is the alarming UNICEF report about the situation of children in Eastern Europe and the former Soviet Union,[29] saying that the situation for the majority of the 150 million children in Eastern Europe has deteriorated massively since 1989. Among the eight million war and civil war refugees are more than two million children, accord-

---

28.   Neues Deutschland (ND) 29th April 1999
29.   Neues Deutschland (ND) 5th November 1999

ing to the UNICEF report. Not only had twenty-six million people lost their jobs, but the wages (real income) were shrinking every year, and in ten years time were halved, forcing families into poverty. Typical poverty-related diseases like diphteria, tuberculosis and others, spread again after decades in which one believed that those epidemics were history.

Most East European states and Russia cut down social and educational spending, a growing number of children do not attend any school. According to specialists, the Russian population will shrink in the next fifteen years by twenty-two million, due to TBC, AIDS, alcoholism and drug adiction as well as other diseases. Moreover, infant mortality has risen since 1999 by 20 per cent. Only every fifth infant is healthy at birth.

Most of the problems stem from the Yeltsin era and not, as most history books will make us and future generations believe, from the Soviet System. Russia's foreign debt climbed up to 160 billion U.S. dollars, which was the gross domestic product of 1999,[30] although people earned less or even lost their jobs and although the social system was destroyed. Already in 1998 Russia had to use some 30 per cent of its income to retire loans, while the Russian Federation was sometimes able to pay only interest and not retire the principal of the loan. By 1999 this quota rose to 38 per cent. In 2001 it was 47 per cent. It will soon reach 50 per cent, and what will come after that is unpredictable. A country the size of Russia, a nuclear power, a country of some historic relation to the revolution, won't think twice if it only takes to overthrow the government if this means that foreign debt and basically interest rates foreign banks imposed on Russia while its people are already starving again, a situation Russians didn't find themselves in for most of the second half of the 20th century, could be eliminated. But as long as politicians like Yeltsin were supported by western banks and the oligarchy Russian mafia, it was certain that the pressure made by banks associated with the Club of Paris was enabling western indus-

---

30.   Frankfurter Allgemeine Zeitung (FAZ) 14th April 2000

tries, especially in the energy sector, to press for privatization and selling off to the West. The European Children's Trust in London found in a study entitled "The Silent Crisis" that "poverty in the region has increased more than ten-fold over the last decade because of reductions in government expenditure on health, education and social provision. Since the breakup of the Communist system, conditions have become much worse...For all its many faults, the old system provided most people with a reasonable standard of living and a certain security." [31]

The IHT[32] speaks of fifty million children in the former Soviet Union living in poverty and facing a hungry winter. And they quote the report saying: "The economic changes for the region from command to market economy has not been a transition but a meltdown." In Central Asia and the Caucasus the economic problems are worse than in the twenties of the last century in Germany. And this is exactly were the new wars in the nineties and today start. These armed conflicts are about access to raw material and natural resources like anywhere else in the world where American industries try to get a foot in the door. Especially, the Caspian Sea region is believed to house more than a third of the world's natural gas reserves, and while the Americans concentrate on the oil fields on the Caspian Sea as well as the Persian Gulf, the Germans focus on the natural gas exploration of the Tengiz field at the Caspian.[33] The same applies for Australia's and Germany's ambitions in Indonesia. No wonder that Bali was the center of the terror attack in October 2002, giving the Australian government a reason to increase their presence there. Australian troops are stationed there for years as "peacekeepers," but are reportedly not behaving like that. Germany, so far, has been represented in Indonesia only by a small number of soldiers, most of them involved in so-called "humanitarian aid" programs. While it appears that Australia and Germany don't have to fear real rivalry when going after the natural gas reserves

---

31. Richard Carter, author
32. 12th October 2000
33. Frankfurter Allgemeine Zeitung (FAZ) 30th November 2001

in Indonesia, the situation at the Caspian Sea is slightly different. The Clinton administration had put much effort in sidelining both Russia and Iran by promoting the multilateral agreement on a natural gas pipeline from Dauletabad (Turkmenistan) via Kandahar (Afghanistan) to Quetta and Multan (Pakistan) a rather adventurous project compared to the initial intentions the Turkish government had in mind when discussing a much more economical way through Iran. Partners to this agreement, which has been executed between Turkmenistan and Pakistan in Islamabad on 23rd July, 1997, were also the U.S.-American oil company UNOCAL as well as the Saudi Arabian DELTA Corp. Four years before the September 11-attacks a military maneuver took place in Kasachstan involving the U.S., Turkey, Kazakistan, Turkmenistan and Uzbekistan. The German economic weekly Wirtschaftswoche on 11th September, 1997, quotes the then vice secretary of state, Strobe Talbott as saying that the "solution of conflicts are the pre-requirement for, as well as result from, any exploration of energy resources." No one seems to even consider what the Russian position must have been when observing a military maneuvre in their hemisphere designed to make them shudder if not feel threatened while being excluded from any agreement for exploration of oil and gas fields in the Caspain region. How strange must the Russians feel about the invitation of the Bush administration after 11th September, 2001, to join them to go to war in Afghanistan, exactly twenty years after the Americans started their semi-secret destabilization process by supporting the last all-Afghani-government in provoking the Soviet Union, which led to the brutal war of the eighties. And now, two decades later, the same Americans ask the Russians to join them? Of course, it has to be seen in the light of the pipeline venture described above.

The Handelsblatt realistically asserts that this would require that the fundamentalist Taleban put the north of Afghanistan under control and make it safe for such an undertaking. [34]

---

34. Handelsblatt 27th July 1998

This may explain why the U.S. administrations of the past decade have always supported the Taleban and have put some faith in them bringing "peace" to that region. Delicate but not very much criticized so far is the fact that the close U.S. ally, Saudi Arabia, paid for the weapons delivered from Pakistan to the Taleban.[35]

Once the U.S. lost that conviction, they dropped their support for the Taleban and just waited for an excuse to get rid of them, one of the main goals during the campaign they entitle "war against terror."

The FAZ states that because of its geographic closeness, Europe should be very interested, they write, and criticise the EU for acting so slow while the oil reserves in the North Sea come to an end, and that with its new East European members, which all do not have any access to oil or gas resources, would be a large market, especially for gas, which would be a clear advantage in the competition between the EU and North America.

In fact, it took the EU another three years to sign a strategic deal with Russia to supply oil to the West.[36] EU president Prodi said in an interview that, "our goal is to expand the zone of stability to Russia itself, so that all of our citizens feel safer…We want to change the commercial relationship into a long-term strategic partnership, which is in the interest of all parties."

And in this interview Prodi speaks out what everyone feels, that Russia has the capacity to be the world's largest oil producer, which would pay off Russia's debts and get Moscow to contribute to European security. In this sense the "energy-bridge between East and West" has been one of Europe's and especially Germany's most elusive geopolitical goals, as the IHT notes. This was the case when Hitler was trying to expand his "Reich" to the Caspian region sixty years before. If he had succeeded, one wishes to add, this could have lead to a different result of the Second World War, at least it could have prolonged it,

35.   Handelsblatt 13th January 1999
36.   International Herald Tribune (IHT)21st/22nd October 2000

because if the Nazis had been in control of such energy reserves, which the Russians at the same time would no longer be able to access, the Red Army would not have had enough oil to fuel their tanks to get them to Stalingrad and defeat the Germans. A horrible and unthinkable scenario. Even more should we be aware of it nowadays when the same ambition with different means comes into effect.

3

Three times in 100 years

1. A thousand-year-old hegemonial dream and phantasy finally comes true.

The Transport Corridor Europe, Caucasus, Asia (TRACECA) is significant for the West European economies; it shall connect Germany and western Europe with Central Asia and the Caucasus. One of its weaknesses was the missing connection between the western end of the TRACECA corridor at the Black Sea with European markets. This has been solved now by corridors IV and VIII connected with the port of Varna. The development projects for the next twenty years for the European continent clearly depend on the realization of these corridors, especially those going through the Balkan region. The central knot of corridors VIII, X and IV form a triangle ranging from Nis to Skopje and Sofia. This triangle is located directly in Kosovo, explaining why Germans and Americans were so interested in "liberating" the ethnic Albanian minority. Any instability in Serbia, Albania or Macedonia would threaten this most ambitious project which may be one of the most important corridor projects in this century. The U.S. showed an unprecedented interest in the Kosovo triangle, and even prohibited a pipeline project, which was to go through Serbia, by offering Romania 100 million U.S. dollars if they moved the route of the planned South Eastern European Line (SEEL) pipeline towards the north, Hungary. The Italian ENI had planned this project by using the already-existing pipelines through Slovenia, Croatia and Serbia. The U.S. bombed particularly this part of the infrastructure. British General Jackson was quoted by the Italian newspaper "Sole 24 Ore"[1] as saying that "it is inevitably necessary to achieve the stability of Macedonia and it's commitment to NATO. We will have to stay here for a long time in order to secure the energy corridors which lead through this country." The paper went on to say that it was "clear that General Jackson meant the VIIIth corridor, the East-West axes, in which a pipeline shall bring the energy resources of central Asia from the Black Sea to the Adriatic. This also explains why all major and medium powers want to participate in finding solutions for this region."

Pipelines in the VIII and X corridor:

In March, 2001, the U.S. Congress discussed the construction of an AMBO oil pipeline from the Black Sea (Burgas) through Bulgaria, Macedonia and Albania to Vlore. This pipeline would supply the U.S. market with crude oil worth 600 Million U.S. dollars per month. There are three possibilities to lay pipelines:

1. Burgas-Alexandrupolis, which would be mainly LUKoil and a Greek consortium who would benefit.

2. Burgas-Vlore, which would be the U.S. AMBO and Halliburton (Cheney's former employer) pipeline.

3. Constanta-Omisalje-Trieste via Romania, Serbia and Croatia (SEEL, ENI, EU interests). Germany and Austria would benefit heavily from this. On the international conference, "Adriatic Pipeline, new perspectives for transport of Caspian oil to the European markets" which had been held in June, 2000, as part of the Inogate program, the third route has been identified as the most advantageous one. The political reasons previously speaking against this concept had been resolved once the Milosevic-government has been removed from power. Croatia would no longer insist on circumventing Serbia via Hungary. At the same time, the U.S. planned the AMBO pipeline in

---

1.   2nd August 1999

the VIII corridor from Burgas via Bulgaria, Macedonia and Albania to Vlore.

The EU has been excluded from any negotiations in this regard.

The VIII corridor had been proposed by the Clinton administration in relation to the Balkan Stability Pact. The infrastructure of this corridor shall be opend for deregulation and privatisation. Although the EU transport ministers suggested use of the VIII corridor, all feasibility studies have been conducted by American companies, financed by the TDA (Trade and Development Agency). The U.S. did whatever it took in order to take over the transport and communication infrastructure of these countries. American companies, such as Bechtel, Enron and General Electric compete (financially backed by the U.S. government) with European companies. Washington's plan had been to open the VIII corridor entirely for American major corporations, in other words let them settle in Germany's economic backyard.

2. Following the Reich's principles.

The government of the Federal Republic of Germany constantly paid about 140 Million German marks for "supporting German Minorities in East, 'Central' and Southeast Europe" per annum. In 1995 it was 143 million DM. Through the following years it has been 140 million.[2]

At least 110 million DM were spent on "Direct support for the German 'minorities' and their abilities to make a living abroad". This describes acts of sovereignity which Germany again executed outside its own borders. The funds were spent on "administrative units in territorries occupied by German nationals.

The fact that those territories were parts of neighbouring states whose inhabitants, respectively citizens, can not legally be governed by German authorities, seemed not to disturb anybody. Due to the minis-

---

2.   Bundeshaushalt 1997 (federal budget), BMI (Ministry of the Interior), Kapitel 0640, page 376.

ter of the interior's never-changed blood line principle definition, people are German if they have a certain proof of ancestry. That's why the German budget reserved such funds to be paid "for German-occupied regions or future regions to be occupied by Germans." Indeed, this follows the ancient NAZI policy and ideology, and the German government not only did not distance itself from such heritage but even enforced it in the Kosovo-Albanian conflict in Yugoslavia.

The war was meant to show the good German attitude to fight for minority rights and human rights of others in order to be able to demand the same in future conflicts where populations of German origin were affected, i.e. in the former Soviet Union or France, Beglium, Austria and Italy or Poland.

Relevant funds are channeled through an organization known as BdN [3] to FUEV [4], which calls itself in English, 'Federation of independent European Nationalities' which does not quite meet the exact translation nor does it reflect the meaning of the German term "Volksgruppen". Let me quote what the U.S. State Department wrote with good reason in 1943: "The 'Volk' (as the Germans again are defining it) is an obscure, compelling, natural entity, bound together by blood and common culture. It is entirely different from our notion of 'people', the social community of citizens having an open, conscious, and optional allegiance to a political union of their own making. The 'Volk' is rather conceived, on the one hand, as a natural organism and as such exerting a compulsory hold on the individual through blood relationship and, on the other hand, as a supernational being, imposing an absolute claim for loyalty and allegiance." [5]

The Federation of European Nationalities (Folkgroups) is nothing else than an ancient German foreign policy tool, an organisation

---

3.   Bund deutscher Nordschleswiger/Federation of German North Schleswig people

4.   Föderation Europäischer Volksgruppen/Federation of European Folk Groups (bloodline principle)

5.   Special Unit of the Divison of European Affairs, Washington, 1943. Seite 67, Raymond Murphy, National Socialism.

reflecting the NAZI policies of the twenties and thirties of the twentieth century, following the ideology of racists. Their aim was to let it supersede by a socalled European Centre of Minorities (ECM) which sounds much more civil.

In fact, the FUEV support meant to employ the racist and fascist policy of the dark German past. And, indeed, Schröder's claim for 'continuity' is also reflected in saying that "Germany calls itself a Great Power" again,[6] as well as former Chancellor Kohl's presumption that "Germany has concluded from its history that it may now openly demand a leading role in world policy." [7]

Schröder, as well as previously Kohl, supported FUEV by state funding, although this organisation had its roots in NAZI organizations. And whereas the authors of said State Department memorandum emphasised the blood line principle of the term "VOLK," they described acurately the racist meaning of such and reflected these in the terms racial or folk community as well as racial corpus.

According to its own publications (article 3 of the memorandum), FUEV demands the creation of an internationally recognised "Volksgruppenrecht", a right for folk groups and minorities, and it even refers in its own statements to the well-known minority-groups of the thirties of the last century. Moreover, it claims to be the legal representative and heir of such groups whose links with the NAZI government is historically evident. [8]

The magazine of this particular institution, "Nation & Staat" (Nation and State) in 1932 (publishing year six), dealt with the segregation of Jews, while the magazine of the FUEV, "Europa Ethnica", published in it's 18th year in 1961 (!!) even publicly states on its front

---

6. International Herald Tribune 13 September 1999
7. "Deutschland hat mit seiner Geschichte abgeschlossen, es kann sich künftig offen zu seiner Weltmachtrolle bekennen und soll diese ausweiten. " Helmut Kohl, federal chancellor, original quotation of statement made in the German Bundestag file No. 29287/1991).
8. "Information. Föderalistische Union Europäischer Volksgruppen", Generalsekretariat, Flensburg, page 4

page that it stands in the tradition of the NAZI paper "Nation & State". It advanced to become the most prominent paper for organisations like "Union of Germanhood Abroad" [9] (Verein für das Deutschtum im Ausland VDA, Bonn), "Hermann-Niermann-Stiftung", Düsseldorf, as well as "Federation of German North Schleswig people" (Bund deutscher Nordschleswiger BdN und FUEV). The paper received annually 10 million marks official support from the federal government, channelled through "Hermann-Niermann-Stiftung". Enormous funds were used for the support of a European Minority and Folkgroup initiative, basically demanding independece for minorities in regions of special interest like Scotland, Wales, Northern Ireland, Alsace, Corsica, Macedonia, Greece, Kosovo, Cataluna, Czech Republic, Eupen-Malmedy (Belgium), Southern Tyrolia, Northern Italy (Padania, Veneto), Basque region, Dutch Friesland, Bretonia, Finland (Samen and Lappen), Kaliningrad (Russia), Romania, Chechnya, and so on.[10]

The German media reflected proudly that the "ethnic principle of minority and folk group protection can be successfully implemented, not only in Europe but also in Asia.[11]

In order to find a way to Europeanize the method of disintegration, and let it appear independent and worthy of support as it claims to be, multinational, European and helping to overcome the division of the European continent and its nations as every European Institution for a while had a positive image, the European Centre for Minorities indeed developed an image of a caring institution understanding and supporting the minorities in a good way.

In fact, the ECM (European Center for Minorities) issues have been founded largely by those German organisations which don't even try to hide their roots in the "Third Reich".

---

9.   Verein für das Deutschtum im Ausland
10. (Budget of the Federal Government, page 379/Bundeshaushalt 1997, Seite 379.)
11. FAZ 13 February 1998

Documents from the Ministry of the Interior make it clear that FUEV had to play a key role in the foundation of the ECM, [12] and as the headquarters of the ECM are in walking distance from the FUEV office in Apenrade, Schlewsig Holstein, there have been intensive synergy effects. Moreover, the former foreign minister, Klaus Kinkel, on 2nd May, 1995, wrote that the ECM operations shall be effectively coordinated through the Foreign Office, department VI and department KII5 of the Ministry of the Interior. [13]

And the government of Gerhard Schröder did not even stop such illegal activities, but even encouraged them and used the ethnic principle the first time after WWII again when claiming to protect ethnic minorities in Yugoslavia. They fall just short of the logical-sounding propaganda of Adolf Hitler when rushing to "defend" German minorities in the Czech Republic of those days. How powerful these groups were one could see when it came to Yugoslavia. The ground has been prepared to "defend minorities" and their drive for independence.

3. The intentional destruction of the Federal Republic of Yugoslavia

Since the beginning of the eighties, reforms imposed by the IMF and World Bank led to social and economic chaos, which resulted in dissolution of the industrial sector and collapse of Yugoslavian social systems. The Reagan administration issued two decisive national security directives, one (NSDD 54) in 1982 describing a strategy to undermine socialist systems in Eastern Bloc countries in order to lead them to a "peaceful revolution," overthrow of communist governments and parties in order to re-integrate Eastern European countries into the world market. The second national security directive (NSDD 133) issued in

---

12. Documents of the Interior Ministry (BMI Dokument für Gründung Europäischen Minderheitenzentrums, 15.10.1993

13. Foreign Minister Klaus Kinkel wrote in a letter dated 02 May 1995 to a MP that the ECM's cross border activities shall be conducted by Departement VI of the Foreign Ministry as well as Dept. KII5 of the Interior Ministry.

1984, entitled "U.S. policy towards Yugoslavia", dealt directly with the Yugoslavian economy. [14]

The consequences of the IMF policy after Tito's death has been dominated by economic and political chaos. Stagnating growth and increasing foreign debt, especially increased payments towards the IMF, as well as the devaluation of the Yugoslavian dinar, lead to a constant decline in the standard of living of the Yugoslavian population. Ethnic adversaries became more visible. Minister President Milka Panic had to agree to the IMF refinancing moratorium, which demanded an increase in the annual retirement of the principal, meaning that Yugoslavia had to pay back its debt faster. This has been one of the Reagan administration's tools. Tensions between the federal government and republics followed. As a direct consequence of the IMF agreement, industrial growth of Yugoslavia declined at a rapid rate because of the deflux of capital. From 1980 until 1987, Yugoslavia was still enjoying an annual growth of 2.8%; from 1987 until 1989 it fell to 0 per cent; in 1990 it fell dramatically to minus 10.6 per cent. The reform for privatising until that time state-owned companies in 1989 had been a central demand of the IMF before they would further "help" Yugoslavia. In 1990 the GDP shrank by 7.5 per cent; in 1991 by 15 per cent., Industrial production declined by 21 per cent. The structural program demanded by the IMF called for further far-reaching privatizations. The profitable exports at the same time stirred the Yugoslavian foreign debt, while its own production collapsed because of a radical opening of the market demanded by the IMF, making any trade barriers obsolete. Drastic increases of the interest rates as well as the raise in the basic costs excluded Yugoslavian companies from their own market and finally led to the collapse.

The World Bank estimated that of 7531 former companies, only 2435 survived until 1990. [15]

---

14. Covert Action Quarterly No. 43 1992/93
15. all data World Bank, Industrial Restructuring Study, Overview, Issues and Strategy for Restructuring. Washington DC June 1991, pages 10 and 14.

Then, the IMF returned to Yugoslavia. The "reform" package in January, 1990, consisted of an IMF moratorium, a so-called stand-by arrangement as well as a structural refinancing facility by the World Bank (SALII). The budget cuts, both, IMF and Worldbank, demanded caused a redirecting of tax revenues of the federal government to retirement of the principal of the loans, while payments from the federal government to the republics were suspended, which accelerated the political dissolution.

The wars between ethnic groups started. These would have started in any other country as well if the IMF had provoked the same economic desaster.

4. How to invade a sovereign country

The best way to start a war these days is by blaming the other side of not complying with democratic standards, of violating human rights and international law. One has to lie of course, otherwise it does not work. In the case of Yugoslavia it has been easy, as President Milosevic has been known over the past ten years by the West as the "Serb in the slaughterhouse." But soon after the NATO war against Yugoslavia, questions arose asking where the "killing fields in Kosovo" were. The private intelligence service "Stratfor" published on 17th October, 1999, a study openly questioning official NATO estimates of more than 10,000 Kosovo Albanians killed. The report finds that there has been no such thing as a ethnically motivated mass-killing of Kosovars by Serbian security forces. The dead bodies found were in the regions of hundreds, not thousands, the report states. According to this report, there were also no mass graves. In this regard, the Rambouillet conference takes a different meaning. Milosevic and his troops had been accused of serious crimes against humanity and ethnic cleansing. In order to avoid further what they say had been human rights violations, Fischer, Schröder and the U.S. pushed for an intervention. Former U.S. secretary of state, Henry Kissinger, later said in Newsweek[16] that "Rambouillet was not a negotiation, as it has always been said, but an ultimatum." And Labor MP Tony Benn went even further, calling the "bombardement of Yugoslavia part of a strategy to destroy and put the Federal Republic of Yugoslavia under U.S. and NATO command. Furthermore, this has been a test whether UNO shall be replaced by NATO. The destruction of Yugoslavia began with the economic reforms, which led to the involvement of the IMF and the pressure forcing the richer republics to leave the federation. Germany and the U.S. officially recognized Croatia, which Genscher called his greatest success. Then Bosnia was targeted, and now Kosovo."[17]

But it was not only the IMF, but also CIA,who operated a long time before the NATO war against Yugoslavia commenced. According to Sunday Times[18] CIA agents were active under-cover, using OSCE camouflage training "Kosovo Liberation Army" (UCK) rebels long before the NATO airstrikes which later had been directed by this terrorist group. In order to maintain public support in Germany, former Defense Minister Rudolf Scharping, a Social Democrat, invented the story of a plan by Serbian forces to eliminate Kosovars by ethnic-cleansing and deportation. This "plan" by the Yugoslavian government of Milosevic was said to be one of the main reasons for NATO's war against Yugoslavia. The TV magazine 'Panorama' of the first German channel ARD later proved that this plan has been invented by the German defense ministry.[19]

Colleague Pfaff of the International Herald Tribune later concluded under the headline, "At last, Reason is now at work in the Balkans" on 2nd October, 2000, that "…The political leaders of the Kosovo liberation army had enjoyed what amounted to the sponsorship of the United States at the time of the February, 1999, Rambouillet conference, preceding NATO's bombing campaign in Kosovo and Serbia. Washington then considered Rugova a marginalized figure and backed

---

16. NEWSWEEK 29th May 1999
17. Neues Deutschland (ND) 29th April 1999
18. Sunday Times, 11th March 2000
19. First German Television (ARD) 18th May 2000

Hashim Thaci, a political of the KLA, whom Secretary of State Madelein Albright advised to become "Kosovo's Gerry Adams," delegating her then press spokesman, James Rubin, "to work with him."

However, when Thaci's KLA arrived in Kosovo in NATO's wake, it seized as much power as it could get, in any way it could get it, and often abused it. These were the new friends of the self-declared "human rights warriors" Schröder, Scharping and Fischer. All this makes more sense when one realizes that the German hegemony expanded when Montenegro introduced the Deutsche Mark as legal tender on 1st November, 1999, "making it possible for the former Yugoslavian republic to further move away from Belgrade".[20]

All this would have been incomplete if Milosevic's grip on Yugoslavian power had not been further undermined. When President Milosevic called for elections in September, 2000, the West's secret services became active again and supported the oppoistion. Under the headline, "A Poll-driven Revolution **'Critical' foreign expertise helped set the stage for Milosevic's defeat.**[21] the IHT noted that "it also marked the start of an extraordinary U.S. effort to unseat a foreign head of state, not through covert action of the kind the CIA once employed in such places as Iran and Guatemala, but by modern election campaign techniques. While the broad outlines of the 41 million U.S. dollar, U.S. democracy-building campaign in Serbia are public knowledge, interviews with dozens of key players in Belgrade and in the U.S. suggest it was much more extensive and sophisticated than previously reported.

In the twelve months after the Budapest strategy session (with students and other activists), U.S.-funded consultants played a crucial role in virtually every facet of the anti-Milosevic drive, running tracking polls, training thousands of opposition activists and helping to organize a vitally important parallel vote count.

---

20. Süddeutsche Zeitung 1st November 1999
21. International Herald Tribune 13th December 2000

Regarded by many as Eastern Europe's last great democratic upheaval, Milosevic's overthrow may also go down in history as the first poll-driven, focus-group-tested revolution.

Behind the seeming spontaneity of the street uprising that forced Milosevic to respect the results of the September 24 presidential election was a carefully researched strategy put together by Serbian democracy activists with active assistance of Western advisers and pollsters." Nothing has to be added.

Forgotten is the fact that Serbs now living in Kosovo, officially still a part of the Federal Republic of Yugoslavia, but under NATO command and a UN protectorate, were unfairly treated, threatend and some of them killed while NATO soldiers were watching. "Serbs in Kosovo facing deadly threats, UN says," the IHT[22] noted. During the UN mission in Kosovo more than 200,000 Serbs were forced to leave the province.

And the FAZ stated that,"the war about Kosovo marked the end of an era for Europe, Russia, the trans-Atlantic alliance and, last but not least, Serbia. After its defeat in the Kosovo war, the economic and political revolution in Serbia, overdue since 1989, had to take place, whether peacefully by free democratic elections or not, remains doubtful." German industries had a unique interest in the "democratic" change in Serbia. As the Ruhr Nachrichten[23] emphasised, "VEW AG and others planned to access EU development and reconstruction funds for former Yugoslavia as well as funds from the World Bank in order not to be left behind U.S. enterprises, once business resumes."

On the other hand, British businesses expected the same. They didn't want to be outmaneuvered by the Germans in Bosnia. German industries held position three in Bosnia, while the British were only listed with "others" as the Confederation of British Industry (CBI) complained, and demanded that Westminster would establish a task force for British interests—economic interests, of course.[24] Another

---

22. 20th February 2001
23. daily circulation Ruhr Nachrichten (RN) 10th June 1999

field where British and U.S. industries were cut out had been the oil pipeline from Constanta (Bulgaria) to Trieste (Italy) via Hungary, Slovenia, Croatia and Serbia, which the German-Italian oil company ENI could arrange for.[25] The only difficulty they saw, according to ENI president Moscato, was the Serbian part of the pipeline, as there were major security issues involved, the paper cited. Well, after Milosevic had been unseated, no such "threats" existed anymore. Under this aspect, appendix B of the Rambouillet "peace" accord takes a new meaning, as NATO called for occupation of all of Yugoslavia at that time, a move rejected outright by the Yugoslavian government of President Milosevic.

---

24. Frankfurter Allgemeine Zeitung (FAZ) 14th June 1999
25. Handelsblatt 13th October 1998

4

The German Cause

1. German military expansion

At the same time, while President Milosevic was taken out of office and soon later handed over to the UN war crimes tribunal in The Hague which is having a hard time to convict him for what he claims was his duty to defend his country, the Germans were heading for their first international leading role in a 'peacekeeping' mission. Without any resistance by the British and Americans, the Germans took over the highest command in Kosovo, a step that had been unthinkable earlier when U.S. and British troops were not involved elsewhere. The German and Dutch brigade also took over the UN command in Afghanistan, but that doesn't mean much more than providing policing and medical aid; it would not give them control over American and British-operated air bases. As in the Yugoslavian wars before, the UN has been sidelined, and the dirty job will be done by everybody else but the Americans.

The Germans soon got what they always wanted: The new NATO mission under German command.[1]

Now, as it appeared to be possible for BP-AMOCO and Texaco-Chevron to lay the pipelines accross Afghanistan, a much preferred route, they could easily give up their dominant role in the Balkans. The Germans, on the other hand, were left all of a sudden in an economically uninteresting but still difficult and hazardous spot.

---

1.   www.spiegel.de/politik/deutschland/0,1518,159410,00.html).

Of course, the Germans had some interest in the Balkans even if the piplines were not laid accross Yugoslavia, but the possibilities of financing the resconstruction and rebuilding of the war-torn area gave less room for exploitation for German industries than expected. Therefore, Chancellor Schröder pressed EU leaders to accept his approach in regard to military participation of European countries in the Afghanistan venture.

Under the headline, "Europe discovers a single voice," the FT reported on 5th October, 2001, that "…It is only a matter of weeks since Mr. Schröder cast aside a half century of German inhibitations to take the lead in Macedonia. Now, for all the political trouble it would cause him at home, the chancellor is ready to commit German forces to the war against the Taleban. Washington's reluctance so far to take up the offer of anything more than intelligence and logistical support does nothing to diminish its significance."

Now, having deployed troops in Yugoslavia the Germans are where they have been two times before in the past hundred years. Even before the Afghanistan War of the U.S. and Britain started, Schröder was eager to find a place for Germany and Europe in this venture. The International Herald Tribune wrote on 20th September, 2001, that, "Schröder urges Europe to stand against foes," while putting much emphasise on Germany's new leadership role in Europe. It is by mere economic might that the other European nations are abiding to what Germany suggests. They are not able to resist any German demand, as the EURO, along with the German industry and banks, control the rest of Europe. At least there has been much disagreement between the European partners on the right strategy. Especially, smaller members were reluctant to declare the "ultimate solidarity" Schröder was vowing on behalf of Europe. It took the Germans a full business day to convince Dutch Prime Minister Wim Kok that it was inevitable to stand by the Americans and even invoke Article 5 of the NATO treaty. The Taoisieach of Ireland, Bertie Ahern, for instance, spoke quite critical of the planned U.S. bombardement, although he was ready to offer Shannon airport for military transport flights. That, indeed, has been very Irish. Two weeks after the attack the Taoisieach still said on RTE radio that bombing a starving people does not solve problems, and that bombs don't create a new world order, but destroy one.

Just a week later the Americans made it clear that the peace talks in Northern Ireland could be at stake again. The Taoisieach calmed down and became a good ally.

The Irish Times reported from the EU summit in Ghent, Belgium: "EU leaders differ on defeat of Taleban. European Union leaders have reaffirmed their support for the military campaign against Afghanistan, but drew back from calling for the overthrow of the Taliban regime. And the leaders watered down proposals for a European arrest warrant by agreeing that it should only be used for terrorist and other serious offences. Last night's summit in the Belgian city of Ghent was over-shadowed by a row over the decision by the French, German and Brit-ish leaders to meet privately beforehand. The British prime minister, Mr. Tony Blair, President Jacques Chirac of France and the German Chancellor, Mr. Gerhard Schröder, insisted that the meeting con-cerned military aspects of the campaign in Afghanistan that did not affect other member-states. But other leaders were clearly annoyed by what they saw as a mini-summit of the three biggest member-states and Portugal's Mr Antonio Guterres condemned the meeting roundly. "Europe should be discussed as a group of fifteen. I don't want to make groups within the EU. The fifteen should work together to find a con-sensus in the fight against terrorism," he said.

This article expresses the rift between major EU countries who have interests in the region of the bombing and those who don't. On the other hand the Taoisieach emphasised that there was no need for changing legislation in EU because of the Afghanistan War of the Americans. The EU arrest warrant, which shall make it possible for German judges to investigate in any other member state (and it's highly unlikley that any Danish, Dutch, Spanish or Irish judge would make use of the same privilege when it came to Germany) and issue arrest warrents even in minor cases, was resisted by a number of nations, including Italy, although in this case driven by personal interests at stake for Minister President Berlusconi of Italy. A few weeks and some back-door "negotiations" later, the only one still being critical of the proposal was Berlusconi, for obvious reasons. The Taosieach has "learnt" in the meantime that if he ever wanted to get away from British rule in the North he had better stick to what the Germans say, and was silenced.

While at that time German Defense Minister Rudolf Scharping urged a "measured response" immediately after 11th September, 2001, NATO invoked Artcile 5, "marking a policy shift" as the Financial Times[2] noted. A NATO diplomat was quoted in the FT, stating that "Besides terrorism, it includes sabotage and organized crime, as well as the disruption of vital resources that could affect the alliance's interests." NATO's perception of its own security interests was rapidly changing; it became much broader, and especially the German government was pushing for this. They might have had in their mind that they wanted to change the German basic law in regard to the domestic use of the German Bundeswehr. Armed forces will soon enhance the policing state of Germany, all in the light of "fighting against terrorism". "Social Democrat" Gerhard Schröder used the opportunity of the moment in order to change the German habit of a low profile security system, and lead Germany in a policing state. By advocating this agenda, Chancellor Schröder sidelined the conservative opposition, who usually would support such ideas.[3]

He has managed to let the development appear inevitable. "Germany becomes a party in a war because the federal government had actively sought such a role."[4], the conservative Handelsblatt asserted.

When Schröder called for a vote of confidence on the Afghanistan war "…Mr. Schröder has staked his reputation on shaping a Germany

---

2.   17th September 2001
3.   Neue Zürcher Zeitung (NZZ) 3rd November 2001
4.   Handelsblatt 6th November 2001

that will be responsible to its allies and take a leading role, military as well as economically, in Europe and the Atlantic Alliance...The war in Afghanistan and his promise of "unlimited solidarity" with the United States have given Mr. Schröder a chance to shatter one of post-war Germany's taboos: that its soldiers could only serve to defend German soil."[5]

This is unprecedented in our post-war history, and it is remarkable that it was a social democratic chancellor and a green, formerly pacifist, foreign minister who actively supported the war. A conservative government would have sparked much more resistance from social democrats, greens and unions, as well as voters.

There would have been a public outcry if former Chancellor Helmut Kohl of the Christian Democrats had sent 3,900 German soldiers into an illegal military intervention, especially when not being asked by the U.S. government to assist, as Defense Secretary Rumsfeld made clear on 7th November, 2001.[6]

The peace movement, once powerful, had been put to sleep by Foreign Minister Joseph Fischer, while parliament was sidelined by Schröder. Of course, the federal constitutional court in Karlsruhe supported Schröder in its decision ruling that, "The government may in principle agree to alterations in international treaties, such as a change in NATO strategy, without Parliament approval", writes the IHT on 23rd November 2001.

In the domestic policy battle, the Schröder government won public opinion on a new policing law. "About the dangers of new state intrusions into private life, especially poignant, given Germany's history," the IHT noted on 1st October, 2001, and went on saying that, "there is also a new mood, reflected in last week's vote in the city state of Hamburg, to get tough on crime. A local judge, Ronald Schill, won more than 19 per cent of the vote in Germany's most sophisticated city, with a new party committed to cracking down hard on criminals, foreigners

---

5.   International Herald Tribune (IHT) 14th November 2001
6.   Westdeustche Zeitung

and illegal immigrants." And although this rightist Mr. Schill has been thrown out of office little time later the foundation has been laid in Germany's political landscape that issues he put forward gained a certain acceptance and are seen by many voters as political correct. That has been probably the only purpose why the German media, especially magainzines like DER SPIEGEL and tabloids like BILD Zeitung offered him a platform. Once he had served the purpose they dropped him like a hot potatoe.

5

Bush's WOILDWAR

1. Psychological warfare

When Ari Fleischer, White House spokesman, said two weeks before the U.S.-Woildwar against Iraq started, that a war on Iraq could be averted only if Saddam Hussein not only disarmed himself but also stepped down, it was not entirely clear whether this had been a Freudian mistake or whether this statement had been authorized by Bush. The later would make sense, although it has never been backed by any of the eighteen UN resolutions dealing with Iraq. The U.S. have been able to dimish the Russian and French advantage in dealing with Iraq only once the Iraqi dictator and his Baath party were unseated, and Iraq occupied.

The French as well as Russian oil industries for many years had already-existing contracts about the exploitation of Iraq's oilfields in their pockets and waited only for the UN to lift its embargo.

Therefore, it made perfect sense that the U.S. sought an UN security council resolution in order to invade Iraq, which would ultimately lead to the overthrow of the Saddam regime. This was already the U.S. strategy in the early nineties, but it had been less pursued, as the Clinton administration was benefiting from the "e-business boom," and would not have to expand internationally. On 16th September, 2002, the U.S. made another effort to focus the UN on Iraq. A month later, UN resolution 1441 followed and threatend Iraq for any false statement or non-compliance with "serious consequences" whatever this should mean. Saddam sent piles of files to New York and led inspectors through any hidden corner of his country, while the U.S. appeared to be uninterested in any of the results of such inspections and sent warship after warship into the gulf region. Secretary of State Colin Powell had to experience a major setback when the IAEA chief, Mohammad al-Baradei, suggested that the documents used by Powell in his multimedia show in the UN Security Council meeting on 8th March, 2003, were faked documents and that his agency had no indications of the Iraqi government or anybody else trying to purchase weapon-grade uranium from Nigeria. The letter Powell showed as proof was a facsimile copy and bore the signature of the foreign minister of Nigeria, but he was no longer in office at the time the letter was written. Moreover, the letterhead was not authentic. Powell tried to appear unimpressed when confronted with his lies. "I got better informations than the inspectors, and I also think that I have more access to information than they have," he said after the Security Council meeting. Even Powell no longer pretends that he believed in his lies. Meanwhile the FBI launched an investigation into how the faked documents got into the hands of the State Departement. Today, we know that the Italian secret service in an attempt to justify military action in which Berlusconi wanted to participate had produced the fake documents.

While the documents handed over by the government of Iraq on 17th December, 2002, describe how more than eighty "daughter companies" of the German industry, among these Daimer-Chrysler, Bayer Leverkusen, Schering and MBB, actively were involved to build up the regime's nuclear and chemical weapon's program since 1975, of which the federal government had detailed knowledge, as well as twenty-four U.S.-owned companies since 1980, aiming in holding position two in the list of weapons suppliers sponsored by now U.S. Defense Secretary Rumsfeld, the governments of Great Britain and the United States of America reached out to "dismantle" the nuclear and chemical weapon's program of Iraq by demanding information about the weapons that their own and Germany's industry delivered to the regime. What a bitter joke as we know today there weren't any weapons of mass destruction, even though US and British troops tried hard to find some. It is hard to believe that Blair believed in his own lies, as the spy-author John Le Carré suggests.

2. US propaganda proves that the power of the media is superior to dictatorships...

I would always prefer that the two leaders waging a war against eachother would not send their soldiers to war but fight the battle by themselves on a chess board. The only reason why I didn't suggest this method in case of Iraq is that I would have hated to see the United States of America been taken over by Saddam Hussein.

Being confronted with the publication of the cruel torture of prisoners in Iraq by US military personell the US had lost any credibility. Not only didn't they find any of the weapons they and the Russians, German and French once sent to Saddam they can not even claim today that they had to get rid of Saddam because he was a cruel dictator. Yes, he certainly was, but does it make a difference to those prisoners whether they are tortured by Saddam's people or by US and British soldiers? The answer is, that yes, it does make a difference because the US and British military command ordered to torture those they said beforehand they would liberate and if not free them at least treat under human rights. It is the moral integrity they claim for themselves but by doing so lost it completely and for a long time. As it has been revealed by an investigation into the Bush-junta's practice they had planned to torture Iraqis before they even conquered the country. Pentagon and White House officials were asked to write an expertise on legal aspects such as how torture would be defined. What the Bush & Rumsfeld advisors came up with is mocking any humanitarian principles. According to the Pentagon documents they considered a person being tortured only if it has been done to him frequently and continously, not if it was only one time, or maybe two times. I would bet that Bush and Rumsfeld and their kind would immediately tell any state secret if they only had their hands being burnt by the glow of cigarettes. A few electric shocks and they would certainly tell their interrogaters what they really knew about 11th September 2001 and who it really was. To think that torture is acceptable when it only occurred occasionally and not every day reveals the real mindset of people like Bush and Rumsfeld. What kind of cowereds and how cynical these gentlemen are is further shown by Rumsfeld's reaction to the media reports about the US-torture prison in Iraq. He said he was angry that these reports have first reached the public and then him. Well, if these reports had reached him first, we can be 100% sure that they would never ever been published. What is making me sick is the fact that the US media manages one more time that the US public forgets the crimes carried out in their name after a few days and that only a minority feels as sick as I do and won't forget. In a way, it is only logic that Bush this time gets elected since it is him who has to finish the job. If he doesn't his dad will be very angry with him and he, like Saddam, won't get any Christmas presents from his parents.

3. Oil and Blood mix

No one seemed to question the inevitability of war. It was only a mere question of time, and in economic research departments of major international corporations as well as in the financial papers, experts were calculating the "return on investment" or how much the war would cost and what would be gained by it. It sounds cynical, but this is how our world is, especially in times of the Bush-Cheney-Rice-bin Laden-junta.

A very convincing return-on-investment calculation we heard from the economic adviser of the White House, Lawrence Lindsey. Although he asserted the "costs" for the war to be roughly 200 billion U.S. dollars, while the Pentagon stuck to their 100 billion, he said the investment is worthwhile, since "a change of regime in Iraq would increase the world's oil supply by three to five million barrels daily." Before the war, Iraq produced roughly 2.4 million barrels per day; in better times it had been 3.5 million barrels. The Iraqi reserves are about 112.5 billion (!!!) barrels; after Saudi Arabia, which accounts for a quarter of the world's oil reserves, Iraq is number two in the Middle East. The production cost in the gulf region are lower than in any other part of the world, between 1 and 5 U.S. dollars per barrel. The black gold is currently sold at the price of more than 30 U.S. dollars. By taking over power in Iraq (or by only implementing a U.S.-friendly government) the U.S. and Britain, whose oil industry before the woild-war did not enjoy good access at the gulf, would control 11 per cent of global oil production directly, in addition to their reservoir before the war. By bombing and occupying Iraq, the U.S. and Britain also bene-fitted from reconstruction contracts, which they have been already negotiating with Vice President Cheney's former employer, Hallibur-ton, and others well before they attacked Iraq. The EU at first said they would withhold reconstruction funds. What Fischer and Villepin did not say, of course, was that because only American and British compa-nies were to benefit from the reconstruction of Iraq, the EU won't commit any funds. Especially, since it is a known fact that the U.S. is suffering from a trade balance deficit, a performance deficit, as well as a budget deficit, it has become clear that only the U.S. and Britain (and maybe some of the "coalition of the willing" which Spain left soon after the ousting of Aznar) will benefit from the woildwar.. "A success in the war on Iraq," Lindsey says openly, "would be good for the U.S. economy."

The chairman of Cambridge Energy Research Associates, Daniel Yergin, was also happy: "A new regime in Iraq would change the bal-ance of power in the whole region." The American interest in that area is even more important, since their old ally, Saudi Arabia, which Kiss-inger once called the fifty-first state of the U.S., acquitted their uncon-ditional fellowship. One reaction had already been Cheney's "New Energy Program," dated summer, 2001, which focused on the Caspian Sea before the Taleban and Osama bin Ladn became a world-reknowned problem. Having the bastion of Afghanistan as cockpit, the

Persian Gulf also became a goal easy to conquer, at least that's what these guys thought. The next goal was Iraq, the others were Iran and the middle East. The high cost Lindsey justifies with the U.S. troops to be stationed after their victory in order to guarantee that "democratisation" of Iraq really pays off for the right ones. Until today, one can say that the US are about to loose the war.

At least there are a few other interests in Iraq: The French TOTAL, the Italian ENI as well as LUKOIL from Russia and a couple of corporations from China and India also had contracts with Iraq and the exploitation of Iraqi oild fields as soon as the UN lifted its sanctions. Of course, this kind of dreaming in technicolour had been proven illusory once the Bush-warriors had put a marionette-government in place.

Even outside the enegry sector the competition is well alive. The German exports to Iraq increased by 46.6 per cent in the first three months of 2002. France had been present as well. Russia confirmed in August 2003 that they had signed an agreement for cooperation in the amount of 40 billion U.S. dollars. Without a war, the U.S. would have lost influence in the region significantly. That's explaining Bush's lust and the European Un-lust.

It should not be hard to understand for people on this planet why Germans in their great majority reject wars outright. Given the dark German past, it should also not surprise anyone that Germans are by far more critical of any unilateral military action like the U.S.-British stance on Iraq than any other European nation. However, this does not entirely explain why the German government of social democrat Chancellor Gerhard Schröder and green Foreign Minister Joschka Fischer played the pacifist flute. Like other European nations, such as Spain, Italy and Great Britain, whose governments vowed to back the U.S. war on Iraq, although a huge majority of their populations opposed it, Germans are also used to their government not listening to them. When Germany, after fifty-six years of non-military foreign policy, broke with its self-defense rule ordered by its post-war constitution of 1949, by committing troops as well as military equipment to NATO's seventy-eight-day bombing campaign against Yugoslavia, lacking any UN madate, in spring, 1999, public opinion in Germany strongly opposed it, Schröder and Fischer failed to convince the German people that they were going to "defend human lives, prevent a humanitarian crisis" and "let Auschwitz never happen again" (Fischer), because the real reasons for participating actively in the disruption of the Yugoslavian federation had been seen by many in an emerging new German hegemonial power, getting the Pan European Transport System (PETRA) and its VIII and X corridor under its influence, a move which had been largely rejected by the majority of Germans. In the aftermath of 11th September, 2001, Schröder and Fischer again said they were only responding to U.S. demands to support their so-called "war against terror" when committing German Bundeswehr troops to be stationed in Afghanistan. It emerged, however, that "woildwar"-Secretary Rumsfeld was not happy about the German insistence to be part of the U.S-British strategy, and millions of Germans were not happy either. Nevertheless the "human rights warriors," Schröder and Fischer, were doing everything possible to "help" the U.S. and "Blair Petroleum" to bring "peace" to Afghanistan. While Germans understood very well the US reaction to the collapse of the twin towers, they also asked why one should bomb a starving people. The pacifist Green and "Social Democratic" government, nevertheless, deployed troops in Afghanistan. As said above, Germans are used to their governments not listening to them.

So why should the Schröder government listen to them now? Well, indeed, there would be enough reason for the German government to endorse the U.S.-British-proposed resolution, as Germany had been named by President Saddam's 12,000-page dossier to the UN in December, 2002, as one of the main weapon suppliers, with more than eighty German companies actively building up Iraq's atomic, chemical and biological arsenal since 1975, a time the U.S., France and USSR were as active in Iraq as West-Germany was. That's why the German government follows the U.S. and Britain in their plea to disarm Iraq. However, they risked being the U.S. 's number-one ally on the continent by insisting that it be done peacefully and not by hysterical military operations, possibly leading to a destabilized world, if not a world war. So why has Germany been with the doves in the UN security council in the wake of the Iraq-war? Why didn't it resist in the same manner the Kosovo and Afghanistan operations, which lacked even more legitimacy for Germany to participate? First of all, Germany, as any other member of the industrial, free market democracies, in its foreign policy is not governed solely by their democratically elected leaders, but by other interests, such as economic pros and cons, advantages and disadvantages.

Whereas the U.S. and Russia are rivals—again or still—the German approach is very different. Since the Germans gave up their oil business by selling it to BP and Shell they had no real interest in conquering Iraq. Also, the reconstruction contracts in their vast majority had been reserved for U.S. companies. The U.S. planned to let Iraqis pay for reconstruction with their own oil, which in theory would be held in a UN-controled fund. The fact that a pro-Bush government had been deployed in Iraq lets this be a farce, of course.

German industries, like the government that bonded their investments, certainly don't want to see the U.S. and Britain bomb these, and they knew that once Iraq had been conquered and is occupied by the U.S. and Britain, Iran will be in the uncomfortable position of being cornered by U.S.-Afghanistan, U.S.-Iraq and the close U.S. ally, Pakistan. And indeed, the US already attempted to destabilize Iran by employing the same technique they once used against President Milosevic: hire students to protest. The world always looks with a lot of sympathy to what students demand in repressive countries. How sad, that the world does not demand the same initiative and does not judge by the same standard when students in Berlin, Washington or London demand that their governments abstain from military interventions. So Iran would be next. The German industry must have feared that the US and Britain would go an shoot the lock while they had their foot in the door already. Even if no other war emerges, the business climate in Iran will change significantly. To put it mildly, German pacifiscm exists only by sheer coincidence, as German industries in a very rare moment have the same interest as the German people: Peace, for different reasons, of course and those war hawks in Washington should reconsider if they ever criticise Germany for it's pacifism as once they started to march again, they might very well march into the wrong direction.

4. The most revealing document in recent US history:

It could certainly be denounced as an obscure conspiracy theory if the signatories to the document were not prominent cabinet members of the Bush junta. The following high-profile politicians wrote a letter to President Clinton, dated 26th January, 1998: Richard B Cheney, today Vice-President of the US; Lewis Libby, Cheney's chief of staff; Donald Rumsfeld, now U.S. secretary of defense; Paul Dundes Wolfowitz, today Rumsfeld's vice-secretary; Peter W. Rodman, today responsible for international security issues; John Bolton, responsible for armament control; Richard Armitage, today vice foreign secretary; Richard Perle, once vice defense secretary under Reagan, today chief of the American Defense Policy Board; William Kristol, chairman of the Project for a New American Century (PNAC), today the key adviser of Bush, and referred to as "the brain" (not responsible for Bushims!) of Bush. Zalmay Khaliza, who used to be special U.S. envoy to Afghanistan and enthroned Karzai as prime minister, had been Bush's man to talk to the Iraqi opposition. In their letter the conspiring "Project for a New American Century" members suggested that only the elimination of Saddam Hussein and a radical change in the U.S. policy with the UN would guarantee that Iraq wouldn't use their arsenal of weapons of mass destruction, which make them a threat to Israel, the U.S. and other states in that region and also an "important part of the world's oil reserves."

They wrote in their letter to President Clinton that, "within a short time, military action should commence, as diplomacy didn't work out. In a long term, the overthrow of Saddam Hussein's regime would be required...We believe that the U.S. has the right under existing UN resolutions to protect our vital interests in the gulf region by military force. In no case shall the U.S. strategy be governd by the wrong antic-ipation of UN Security Council unanimity." The only question that remains is why the U.S. helped Saddam Hussein in his coup in 1979, as they knew already that he was an evil guy, not a democrat, but one who could be used against Iran. Maybe, that was what let him appear to be qualified.

More than ten years ago Wolfowitz and Libby, two hard-liners of the PNAC and today influential members of the Bush administration, advocated the new U.S. strategy in Eurasia. In 1992 they wrote that a country that might threaten the U.S. by the mere possession of weap-ons of mass destruction would have to expect a pre-emtive military action. The traditional alliances such as NATO should be replaced by ad hoc alliances that should be implemented only for a certain time and only for a certain cause. The former British Minister for the Envi-ronment(1997-2003), Michael Meacher, was quoted on 10th Septem-ber, 2003, by THE GUARDIAN as saying that the US airforce between September 2000 and June 2001 in 67 non-hijacking—cases launched their fighter jets when planes, commercial as well as private jets, had lost their course or left the designated route, and guided these back onto the right cruising altitude or forced them to land. Just on 11th September 2001 the US airforce's fighter jets all remained on the ground for several hours. The former Minister goes on quoting from a document from the "Project for a New American Century" dated Sep-tember 2000 in which the Cheney-Wolfowitz-Junta described how dif-ficult it will be to transform the US into the dominating power of tomorrow *unless* a major catastrophic event having a catalyzing effect like Pearl Harbour would happen.

The current U.S. administration, consisting of these people, used "Weapons of Mass *Distraction*" in order to hide their real agenda.

All this had only one goal, manifesting U.S. rule and dominance in the world, while their Iraq-venture with the oil production not been working that well so far seems to be an pre-*empty*-ve strike, compared to what the oil industry had expected.

5. Germany's hidden agenda

The federal government allowed the U.S. military command the use of U.S. military facilities in the Federal Republic of Germany during a war the United States of America launched on 20th March, 2003, against Iraq although Chancellor Schröder previously mainatined that "Germany will not participate in any war activities againt the Republic of Iraq, not even if a mandate is obtained by the United Nations Security Council".[1] Even after the federal election of 22nd September, 2002, Schröder said in his first address as newly-elected chancellor to the 15th German Bundestag on 29th October, 2002, that "we will not participate in any military intervention in Iraq."

When visiting the United States of America on 31st October, 2002, Foreign Minister Fischer altered this stance slightly by excluding "active military participation…while there is nothing like a passive participation". The Frankfurter Allgemeine Zeitung noted that the foreign minister didn't want to discuss the possible use of military bases by the U.S. [2]

At NATO's summit in Prague on 21st November, 2002, Schröder changed the official position of the federal government by saying that, "The federal government will, of course, fullfil it's obligations as an ally, but would not participate in any military action against Iraq." [3]

---

1.   15th September 2002
2.   Frankfurter Allgemeine Zeitung (FAZ) 1st November 2002
3.   website of the federal government on 21st November 2001

In regard to the rights to use German airs pace, Schröder said that the "federal government would not limit the overflight rights for our friends. We are legally bound to do so and we will not refrain from that."[4] At least he still called the US "our friends".

On 27th November, 2002, Schröder said on a news conference that the "Federal Republic of Germany will gurantee the rights of the United States and NATO to use their bases for mobilizsation, transportation and logistically, should they plan to attack Iraq."[5]

Fischer announced on 28th December, 2002, that the federal government, being a member of the UN Security Council, would possibly vote 'yes' in order to endorse a U.S.-led "coalition" carrying out military actions against Iraq. [6]

This means that the federal government planned to support the envisioned military actions of the United States of America against Iraq from German territorry and by use of the German air space, and by this participate in the campaign.

Schröder said on ARD television on 11th December, 2002, that German soldiers will be on duty in AWACS aircraft "in order to protect the alliance's territorry".[7]

The federal government by this planned a direct participation of German military personnel in the war against Iraq. The Frankfurter Rundschau cited that AWACS aircraft are flying military operations, which even when flying in high altitude above Turkey can spy far into Iraqi territorry, more than 500 kilometers away.[8]

The defense spokesman of the oppositional Christian Democratic Union in the parliament, Christian Schmidt, concluded from this fact that "AWACS participation of German soldiers effectively are combat missions."

---

4.   FAZ 23rd November 2002
5.   website of the federal government 27th November 2002
6.   Spiegel online 28th December 2002
7.   First German Television (ARD) programme,Farbe bekennen' 11th December 2002
8.   Frankfurter Rundschau (FR) 13th December 2002

Schröder's offer for the U.S. military command to use bases on the territorry of the Federal republic of Germany as well as manning AWACS aircraft with German military personell violated Article 26/1 basic law by indirect and direct participation of the Federal Republic of Germany by preparing to launch a war of aggression of the United States of America against the Republic of Iraq, and thereby the relevant paragraph 80 of the German criminal code (StGB) which clearly prohibits any such action, punishable by a minimum sentence of ten years and up to life-long imprisonment. This, of course, did not bother the Schröder-Fischer-gang, as their active involvement into the war over Kosovo would weigh heavier than letting the US use the overflying rights to attack Iraq. It is like convicting Al Capone on grounds of tax evasion and not much more serious crimes.

Nevertheless, we have to scrutinise carefully how the German constitution and laws have been violated. It also sheds a light on the "pacifism" Schröder and Fischer have been eager to be seen in in the German public.

Common international law is introduced legally binding into the German constitution by article 25. It says: "The international laws are an integral part of the German federal law, and constitute direct rights as well as obligations for the inhabitants of the Federal Republic of Germany."

One of the common international laws expressly prohibited any use of force (article 2.4 of the UN charter) or even threatening with the use of force, which is to be seen as an unlawful act and aggression. Adopting international law by the German basic law made the plans of the United States of America and its support by the federal government unconstitutional. Especially, Article 26 of the basic law prohibits "any action designed to disturb the peaceful living together of the peoples as well as the preparation and/or launching of a war of aggression, and are punishable under German law."

Luckely, we Germans got a constitution which shall protect us against any violent aggressor holding office. Unfortunately, the constitution is usually not very much quoted in situations were the rulers decide that they want to ignore it. Anyway, it is good to have it at least written down what is right and wrong, especially in a country like Germany, in which even the dinosours could sue the human beings after a potential revolution.

Article 87a of the basic law declares that, "Except for defense, the German Bundeswehr may be used only in accordance with the regulations of this Basic Law" [9]

Article 26 reflects in Paragraph 80 of the German criminal code: "Whoever prepares a war of aggression (article 26 basic law) in which the Federal Republic of Germany shall participate, and by this evokes the danger for the Federal Republic of Germany to be involved in war activities, will be punished by life in prison or a minimum sentence of ten years."

The official announcement of the Federal government to participate in the war of the United States of America against the Republic of Iraq constituted such a crime as described in article 26 basic law, as well as Paragraph 80, German criminal code.

In order to determine whether it has been a war of aggression by the United States of America one has to scrutinise the relevant articles of the UN charter: Article 2, paragraph 4 of the UN charter expressly states that, "all members respect the territorial sovereignity and political independence of all states and abstain from any threatening of or military action or other force."

The definition of a war of aggression reads in the UN resolution A/ 3314 (XXIX) executed on 14th December, 1974, as follows: "A war of aggression is committed by the state which strikes first. Article 3 explicitly mentions the invasion by foreign military into another state, the bombardement or use of any kind of weapon against another state, as well as the military forces of another state."

---

9.   Artikel 87a, Absatz 2, Grundgesetz, Bonn, 23rd May 1949

As per this legally binding resolution, the war by the United States of America constituted a material breach of this resolution and international law.

The above breach of contract also constitutes an illegal act, as defined by article 39, UN charter (chapter VII), which in principal would have authorised the Security Council to take action against the United States of America, as it is a military action against a member state.

Article VII of the UN Charter reserves the right for the Security Council to execute certain military sanctions against a state under specific regulations. Such a resolution did not exist in case of Iraq. Resolution 1441 did not constitute any automatism leading to military sanctions, despite the threat that in case of non-compliance by Iraq with said resolution, the UN Security Council may issue a resolution allowing military action to discipline the regime. However, no non-compliance had been asserted. And, as we know today, Saddam hasn't been not clever enough to hide any weapons of mass destruction but simply didn't have any. He hasn't even been clever enough to hide himself.

General Secretary Annan said on 12th December, 2002, that if Iraq fully complied with resolution 1441 a peaceful solution would have been possible. Of course, the US never took the UN serious unless they won agreement in the security council. The truth is that the leaders of the US and Britain knew that they were telling lies about weapon's of mass destruction supposedly hidden by Saddam, and they knew that we, the rest of the world, knew that they were lying and they knew that we knew that they knew that we knew they were lying and they gave a shit about it and simply went to war although the UN opposed it, Russia, China, France and Germany, many other countries and last but not least almost every thinking person on this planet condemned it but that didn't impress them at all.

6. Participation of the Federal Republic of Germany

In order to determine the exact illegal action undertaken by Chancellor Schröder in regard to the aforementioned crimes, one has to scrutinize Article 3, f) of the definition of aggression, as per UN Resolution A/ 3314 (XXIX), which states that, "the action of a state, which is to be seen in allowing that its territorry, which it offered to a third state, is used by said state in order to commit an attack against another state" violates the UN charter.

Infact, Chancellor Schröder granted the United States of America freedom to fly over German territorry, land on their air bases, which they said they would use for transport and logistics. The Federal Republic of Germany thereby violated UN Resolution 26/25 (XXV), dated 24th October, 1970, as well as UN resolution 42/22, dated 18th November, 1987.

Regarding the government's responsibility in allowing the U.S. military to carry out their attacks from German territorry against the Republic of Iraq, the definition of aggression is of some relevance: Article 3 (f) of Resolution A/3314 (XXIX), dated 14th December, 1974, sees an aggressive act by a state that offers its territorry for another state to attack a third state.

This is true in this case. Former governments of Chancellor Willy Brandt in 1973 denied shipment of U.S. weapons to Israel through the port of Bremerhaven, and in 1986 the Kohl government rejected demands for overflying rights for the U.S. Air Force to Lybia, all this although Germany at that time was not sovereign. In addition, this rejection had been somewhat delicate as German companies had built chemical weaponry factories in Lybia which in 1989 were bombed by the US..

Moreover, the NATO treaty, dated 4th April, 1949, does not have any legal effect in this case. The war of the United States of America against the Republic of Iraq is a breach of article 1 of the treaty, which is expressly based on article 51 of the UN charter. Article 5 of the

NATO treaty allows use of force only in case of a collective defense of the member states after being attacked. According to article 3 of the treaty, each of the members is free to decide how much it can and wants to contribute in such a case.

There was no reason to invoke article 5 of the NATO treaty. So why did Schröder make this offer to the US?

Schröder and Fischer publically claimed that the Federal Republic of Germany was legally bound to support the United States of America in their military action, if this support is granted by the overflying rights as well as maneuvres on U.S. military bases in Germany. They quoted the NATO troop deployment treaty, dated 19th June, 1951, as well as the addendum to said treaty, dated 3rd August, 1959, as well as the latest revision of the addendum, dated 18th March, 1993. However, these treaties regulate the presence, rights and obligations of U.S. military based in the Federal Republic of Germany under NATO command. There is no provision for any military activity not governed by the NATO treaty. The federal government has the right, if required by our constitution, to deny the U.S. any illegal activity. The Federal Republic of Germany has, since 3rd October, 1990, full sovereignity over its territorry. The addendum to the NATO troop deployment treaty has been amended in reference to the Treaty on German Unity, dated 31st August, 1990, as well as the so-called Two plus Four Treaty, dated 12th September, 1990. The federal government in 1993 cited the addendum as "a progressive achievement in regard to the much clearer definition of German sovereignity requiring special permission from the federal government for any military activity by foreign troops deployed in Germany under the NATO treaties." [10]

Due to this addendum to the NATO treaties, even maneuvres are military actions foreign troops carry out and must have official permission by the federal government. If even maneuvres require such special permission military action would as well, no matter what, legal or illegal.

---

10.   Deutscher Bundestag, 12/6477, page 59

Also, acrticle II of the NATO troops deployment act clearly states that German law applies on foreign military bases. German law and the German constitution, our basic law, prohibit any action that is not carried out in order to defend the territorry of the Federal Republic of Germany or, if article 5 of the NATO treaty has been invoked, of our allies.

Article 53 of the addendum expressly states that foreign troops deployed under this act in Germany are bound to carry out only defensive activities. Therefore, the use of bases in Germany by the U.S. military in the war against Iraq violated these treaties as well as German laws and the German constitution.

There is no doubt that under article 57 of the addendum to the NATO troops deployment act, the federal government has to approve or disapprove overflying rights by foreign forces or any kind of movement across German borders.

7. Legal consequences

By actively allowing U.S. forces to prepare for their war against Iraq, the Schröder-Fischer government violated article 26 of the basic law, which in effect is a violation of paragraph 80 of the criminal code. They face life in prison if found guilty. Therefore, and as the war of aggression has been imminent, immediate action by the federal prosecutors had been inevitably necessary in order to prevent the Federal Republic of Germany from becoming a participant in the war, but nothing happend after suits against Schröder & Fischer were filed at the federal constitutional court in Karlsruhe.

Furthermore, by acting collectively, Schröder, by unnecessarily permitting the U.S. military to operate from German territorry, defense minister Struck, by ordering AWACS aircraft to commit to the U.S. war, and Fischer, by advocating a UN resolution in favor of the U.S. war againt the Republic of Iraq, on 31st December, 2002, while backing away from it in due course, the three form a criminal gang.[11]

In the IHT on 13th March, 2003, a week before the war started, one could read that Germany contributed a third of the AWACS personnel. The same paper quoted Fischer in an article headlined "Germans' hopeful message to America: Its nothing personal," assuring the U.S. that "after the war with Iraq was over, and even during the war, Germany will show its loyalty, and that the earlier close relations could be restored."

And the brilliant Joschka Fischer, pacificst from his heart, went on to point out that Germany has made far more of a contribution to its alliance with the U.S. than all the other countries in the 'new' Europe that have sided with Bush. Not much later, Germany announced it would assign 2500 soldiers to guard U.S. military bases, as well as ten Patriot missiles and as many as 1000 soldiers to help defend Turkey in case of a war. They have, of course, not sent the missiles to Turkey directly, as this would have been illegal under German export law, but they sent them to the Netherlands, who sent them on to Turkey. Eventually, the missiles landed were they had been designated to be these days, in Iraq. For several months, fifty German Bundeswehr soldiers were operating the Fuchs Spürpanzer (FOX anti ABC tank) under U.S. command in Kuwait. On 21st March, 2003, they were joined by another hundred troops who may have come under attack, as they were in Kuweit for only one reason: to support the Americans once chemical or biological weapons would have been made use of. It may be seen as a proof that noone really believed that Saddam posed any threat otherwise they would not have stationed German troops alone there with just little equipment. Hasn't Germany been contradicting itself by saying the one thing, and even risking long-time friendship with the U.S. while helping them in Kuwait, in the gulf of Aden, where German marines patrol the gulf at the horn of Africa in anti terror missions, protecting the military bases in Germany, committing a third of the AWACS personnel and granting overflying rights to the U.S.?

---

11.   § 129 and 129 a criminal code/StGB

When one considers that Spain's Aznar pretended to be such a good friend and ally of the U.S., but didn't commit more troops in the current conflict than Germany, one may very well ask why the Germans have such a bad reputation with Americans these days. They may have voiced their doubt about the legitimacy of the Bush-War, they may have tried to block decisions in the UN Security Council, but would they have done so if Washington promised them participation in the reconstruction of Iraq, if not even a share in the oil, although this is less important to German industries?

8. The war is over, but who won?

So what has happened after the U.S. has won over Bagdad and most parts of Iraq? Will they control the oil of the gulf as well as the Caspian Sea, and by this dictate the prices. If they lower the prices, they hurt Russia; if they increase prices, they hurt Germany and Japan. Again, it is also an economic war, a war that in the end will be fought between U.S. capital and European, if not German capital. It is hard to predict who will finally win this war, the U.S. did win over Iraq and Bagdad, but will they win the W(oil)dwar? Very unlikely. The sacrifices on all sides will be enormous. While one can expect a good return of investment for the U.S. in relation to the Iraqi adventure, economically it will be very costly for the U.S. to maintain security, not only in the regions they occupy, but also at home. As the Financial Times on 9th October, 2001, confirmed, the U.S. military-industrial complex clearly profits from the war against Afghanistan. The U.S. defense budget even stirred growth in the stock markets. According to the FT, the U.S. defense budget in the next years will rise to 400 billion U.S. dollars. In 2003 the defense budget increased by 14 per cent, the largest increase in more than twenty years, and for 2005 by 7.1% and now accounts for more than 15 per cent of the total U.S. budget.[12]

---

12.   Berliner Zeitung 25th January 2002

The only industries in the U.S. that benefit from this development are the military-industrial complexes that could celebrate a 74 per cent increase in orders in 2002, and aircraft manufacturers, who enjoyed an increase of 42 per cent in orders in their books. This is the only indication of an economic recovery in the U.S., and a lot speaks for further expansion in this field, while other manufacturers either stagnate or will decrease. Above all, the U.S. currently suffers from three deficits: a trade deficit, a budget deficit and a production deficit. The deficit-spending the Bush administration presently engages in will not trigger any economic boom, as the purchasing power of the American people won't increase by these measurements, and although domestic demand declines because of shrinking wages, increasing unemployement and a desastrous social situation, the production deficit will only contribute to the trade deficit, and in the end the public deficit. America will try to make good on these three deficits with cheap oil they wish to be able to access after Iraq has been pacified, but will the U.S. be able to keep up with its domestic problems or is it more likely that benefits of the Iraqi oil fields will be eaten up by the high security costs as well as the trade deficit (America has to import almost everything these days, and can not meet its shrinking domestic demand, even though this is constantly declining) as well as a weakening U.S. dollar (which they might be tempted to let fluctuate further in order to reduce the deficit), making such imports more expensive and in the end unaffordable. The U.S. will pay a high toll for relying on oil. With the decline of the U.S. in the aftermath of the Woildwar, others will emerge.

In the end, one will see Germany and Russia stand united and rule over Europe, while the economically, psychologically, and morally exhausted U.S. will decline and probably not recover for a long time from the lost "world war against terrorism" they triggered unless the economic system is changed and improved entirely.

9. After Bagdad fell.

Once Bagdad fell the arm-wrestling in the UN Security Council started again, as Russia and France demanded that existing contracts remaind valid, as their indsutries had long time ago closed deals with Saddam's regime, and waited only for sanctions to be lifted in order to materialise their interests. Of course, the U.S. did not move an inch from its position, since the whole purpose of this war had been expansion into the gulf region. Russian, French and German corporations now felt that they were left behind by the British and U.S. [13]

Russian Vice Prime Minister Alexej Kudrin explicitly demanded that "international treaties be obeyed, no matter how Iraq will be structured and governed after the war."

Also, the Russian energy minister made it clear that he expected Russian companies to return to Iraq. In January, 2003, the Russian oil consortium Soyusneftegaz had acquired drilling rights on the Rafidain-field in southern Iraq, now occupied by British troops. Of all known Iraqi oilfields, Russian companies had secured some 60 million barrels. Lukoil, Russia's largest oil company, is said to have invested 4 billion U.S. dollars, while Tetneft from Tatarsan had secured thirty-three Iraqi oil wells. More than sixty new contracts were ready to be signed just before the war. "This war destroys Russian interests," the former Russian energy minister, Schafranik, is quoted. Not only oil companies will be hit hard by the loss, but also suppliers of drilling technology will struggle to compensate their losses.

Russia had been one of the key clients during the embargo, buying 40 per cent of the Iraqi oil under the oil-for-food program, and delivered goods in exchange for which the world market would be quite limited.

France had similar interests at stake in Iraq, as French industry had been the main trading partner of Iraq for many years. The Iraqi market offers a huge potential for telecommunication, roads, railway tracks,

---

13.   Handelsblatt 01st April 2003

cars, everything that has been destroyed in the war. "French companies want to go back to Bagdad".[14]

German industry did not expect anything from a post-war Iraq under U.S. control. It is evident that German companies had been sidelined because of the German government's resistance to the U.S. invasion, the German industrial federation asserted. Infrastructural programs, worth multi billions of Dollars, and financed by Iraqi oil, have been awarded only to U.S, British and Australian companies, the coalition of the willing, so to say.

For British industry, loyality of the Blair government to the Bush junta will pay off very well. The logistics company P&O, as well as British construction companies, Amec and Balfour Betty, will rebuild the port of Umm Kasr. In order to acchieve this, the state-run Iraqi oil company will be privatized and by this the clock be set back to the time before 1972, when the British Iraq Petroleum Co. had been forced to wind down.

---

14.   Handelsblatt 26th March 2003

6

The European Dream

1. Paving the Way

As early as in 1995 the discussion about the necessity for creating a European constitution started in Germany. What is the true aim of these politicians who talk about the new Unity of Europe, it's values, the basic human rights everyone in the new Europe would enjoy. What is it we can expect from a European constitution which our present constitutions in all our countries are not able to guarantee us? What should make everybody suspicious is that those people who advocated the wars in Yugoslavia and later threw bombs on civilians now talk about the constitution as something inevitable, finalising the unification of the new European Union. They make it appear like a logic democratic process which should make all Europeans happy. And in fact, the media supports this process by creating a general mood and political correctness. If one wants to appear on the hight of the times and modern one has to be pro-European because everything else would be seen as narrow minded, nationalistic, chauvenistic and ignorant. The media in all countries of the EU also manages quite well to pick up the criticism from citizens over certain laws and regulations apparently being drawn by Brussels in order to let it appear an open democracy, seeming to understand it's citizen's worries and listening to them while the politicians are in the comfortable position to refer to the anonymous beaucracy in Brussels which they say is responsible for crack down on social welfare, neoliberal agenda and militarisation. It is far more easy to criticise "Brussels" as it stands for a mega power no national leader, government or parliament can do anything against. The citizens in various EU countries may be angry about "Brussels" but then again, it is far away from most of them except for the Belgians maybe but even they keep their distance. National politicians in all member states have already understood quite well that they can divert the anger which usually unloads over them to "Brussels", the EU's mega beaucracy which as hated as it may be still represents the image of the only solution after two world wars and painful seperation in the aftermath of WWII. Should one not wish to be seen anti-european or narrow minded one has to be in favour of the new Europe, its ultimate unification and not ask those stupid questions like who is going to profit from the expansion. As far as the new members are concerned the expectations there were high but they will soon see that there middle class entrepreneurs will face bankruptcy as the German industry wants to and will sell their products and eradicate the Czech, Hungarian, Polish or Lithuanian products. And the peoples in "old" member states will realise that while their giant industries like Siemens AG who increase there profit expectations because of the European expansion will shut down factories in the West and move to the East because of the cheaper labour costs and an additional subsidy they get from Brussels for moving there. In other words, our taxpayer's money will be used by "Brussels" to lower standards and wages for those who work for major companies moving to the East leaving behind unemployment in the deserted regions of Europe while not creating much more than an artificial boom in the countries they move to.

This is also true for the multinational companies who one after the other will move to the new member states and request the same subsidies again which they had already received when moving to Ireland. Now, as most Europeans may not be aware of the content of the draft constitution we will examine a few of the most striking issues as the neoliberal agenda laid by the Maastricht austerity criteria will now be blessed by becoming a "human right". How cynical it is to describe the crackdown on social rights, environmental standards and cultural acchievments as "human rights" while committing to a dreadful profit maximisation logic proven to be desastrous throughout the world, from Japan to Russia, Mexico, Argentina and the United States of America and the simultane militarisation of the EU's foreign and security policy, becomes obvious when one scrutinises only some of the Articles of the new constitution.

Let's first have a look on the composition of the "European Convent". Andreas Wehr, who followed the process closely as he participated in it as an advisor to the leftist fraction GUE/NGL, painstakingly scrutinised every aspect of the composition of the Convent as well as the draft constitution. How is it possible that respected politicians from all member states commit themselves to a neoliberal agenda and undemocratic principles if they were representing their parliaments and have not been extremists in those? The largest group of representatives have been 30 members of parliaments of the member states, the European Parliament accounted for 16 representatives and one per country, i.e. 15, have been delegated by the 15 governments. In addition there were 2 representatives of the European Commission and the President of the Convent and his two Vice Presidents. Also invited have been 26 members of the national parliaments and 13 government representatives of the new member states. In total the Convent counted 105 members, 83% were men. When it came to the question how to guarantee equal rights for men and women one could clearly see that women were under-represented. It is only owed to tremendous pressure from outside that some acchievements in this aspect were made and written down in the new Constitution.

It has also not been commented on publically yet that the "European Convent" had been composed politically absolute homogene and very one-sided as the selection of the representatives of member states, one per government and two per national parliament, in all cases made the largest fractions of a parliament select the representative, i.e. one conservative and one "Social Democrat" or liberal. Therefore, other groups of the political spectrum like the Greens, parties of the left or simply EU-sceptical politicians were left out although with all the EU-scepticism in the societies of all member states they might have been the better representatives as they might have taken the sorrows of the people more serious. Especially the East-Europeans might soon discover that the material their cars used to be made of will be the material their lives are now made of.

In other words, those who decided over the composition of the "European Convent" the European Council, which is only made out of government ministers, prime ministers or presidents, made sure that no critical voices would be heard in the deliberations but the usual conservative and "socialdemocratic" protagonists who already in their national parliaments usually make no trouble but vote as the neoliberal agenda of most of the member state's governments requires.

So, before we go further into detail why the project of the "European Constitution" is a bad idea seen from the perspective of the citizens we have to question the legitimacy of those who say they negotiated over years and months a deal for us citizens being our representatives. Neither have we voted for them, nor has the "European Convent" been composed in a way that would reflect the real political and sociological spectrum in our countries. That fact alone speaks for itself but not for the document these people call the "European Constitution". Because we know that only those who were already willingly if not deliberately participating in the neoliberal crackdown on social-, human- and environmental rights, were drawing this "constitution" for us we are right not to have high expectations but be very suspicious.

So far, there was nobody able to explain to us why such a "constitution" would become necessary. The advocates of it usually say that because Europe became too big by adopting new member states this year and some more in the next years a reform in the decision making process is needed. In fact, one can not really see a benefit in those nightly discussions and armwrestlings in which all governments every half a year try to get a bargain while one minister after the other falls asleep. This is how the European currency project was brought on its way through the Masstricht accord. In those meetings some participants were already sleeping and others physically not able to follow any discussion, some were drunk or under other influence and look where the desaster of the EURO led us to: a stability pact and austerity criteria no government is able to live up to for long even if they crack down on the social system, privatise everything, sacrifice any democratic acchievement and establish dictatorships. If I was wrong, it would not be a fact that even the German government although being the most brutal one in implementing the austerity criteria has to face the sanctions by the European Commission for not being in line with the so called "stability pact".

While the "European Convent"had been dominated exclusively by those politicians who see the neoliberal agenda of the Maastricht accord as something without alternative a significant role by pushing through the agenda was played by the Presidium of the convent, writes Andreas Wehr[1] who witnessed the process closely as an assistant deputy for the Leftist group (GUE/NGL) of the European Parliament. It had been composed by two members representing the national parliaments, two representing the European Parliament, three members representing the national governments as well as the two members of the Commission and the chairman of the "European Convent", French Ex-President Valéry Giscard d'Estaing. It certainly lets one's eyebrowes rise that the European Commission having two seats in the convent also gained two seats in the Presidium. One could ask why but the answer would be diplomatic although it is obvious that the presidium was meant to be controlled by the European Commission which wouldn't like to see any surprises. By this the European Commission had much influence on the work of the convent. All in all, one can say

---

1. "Europa ohne Demokratie?" Papyrossa Verlag Köln, 2004

that only the five big EU countries, France, Germany, Greatbritain, Italy and Spain had been dominating the presidium of the convent. It was the presidium where all decisions were pre-set as the presidium decided over which draft legislation would be delegated to which task group and which ones would be ignored and not even voted on. The task groups were headed by members of the presidium while the various tasks were determined only in this gremium by this already making it impossible for any unforeseen changes or requests even to be submitted. All documents were pre-negotiated in the presidium and in close cooperation with the national governments to which chairman Giscard d'Estaing kept close contact as one of the members of the presidium, Gisela Stuart, a British Labour MEP, wrote in her book[2]. According to Mrs Stuart the European Charta containing our basic rights, which had been drawn under the auspices of German Ex-President Roman Herzog in 1999 and 2000, had been accepted without any changes while any suggestions made from the task group "Social Europe" had been ignored.

Giscard d'Estaing frequently conferred behind closed doors with national governments writes Mrs Stuart. He wanted to get their approval while none of these informal meetings were protocolled, although many members of the convent requested that. This shows that the initial idea to get away from the nightly sessions behind closed doors at the government conferences has been countercarricatured by this presidium.

After more than a year a first draft for merely 16 articles dealing with the administrative structure of the European Union had been presented to the members of the convent. This was on 6th February 2003. Being immensly under time pressure to complete its work until 10th July 2003 it was clear now that if the deadline would have to be meet no detailed discussion would be possible as the third part of the "Constitution" alone counted 342 articles dealing with the security &

---

2.   Gisela Stuart "The Making of Europe's Constitution", publ. by the Fabian Society, London 2003

defense-, judicial- as well as politics of the interior. This draft had been presented to the members of the convent only on 27th May 2003 but the next conference was already to be held on 30th and 31st May 2003, so there was very little time for the members to read and scrutinise these 342 very decisive articles. Still, there were 1,600 suggested changes but the convent had only two more meetings before the final draft had to be presented to the European Council. Therefore, the deliberations became a farce mocking any democratic principles.

2. Streamlining the decision making process

Once the French and German foreign ministers De Villepin and Fischer had submitted their "French-German contribution for the institutional architecture of the EU" it was clear that the future structure of the decision making process was laid and would not be changed fundamentally as France and Germany traditionally were seen as the driving force for European integration and no other member state would really have a say. This is why the chairman of the "European Convent" Giscard d'Estaign only after this French-German initiative had been applauded by the media in both countries presented exactly the same verbiage in "his" draft of said 16 articles dealing with the decision making process of the European Union only after De Villepin and Fischer had presented their's. As this was the most decisive phase in the deliberations of the convent the two foreign ministers De Villepin and Fischer became members of the presidium and it was clear that the members of the convent were not all but equals. When the German foreign minister offered a statement the tv cameras surrounded him, while most journalists left the press conferences when another foreign minister was speaking. The role of the media in this aspect became relevant as only those views which were published had any impact on the decision making process. One has to question the legitimacy of those media preferences and whether these journalists had any morals or whether they were simply instructed by someone to focus on Joseph Fischer who was never hiding his ambitions to become the EU's first elected president. It could well be a mixture of both, pressure from the publishers and editors—in-chiefs, as well as a self-imposed censorship. Other than in open dictatorships such self-imposed censorship works very subtle, especially among freelance journalists who have to sell their news every day, getting paid by printed line. After a few articles which had been rejected by the publisher or editor—in-chief will teach the "independent journalist" how to become a successful story-writer or inventor of the fabrications our media is full of. These media are usually quick to applaud if Fischer speaks of the necessity to getting the decision making process more transparent or even fair. Conflicting views are most of the time overheard as Fischer represents the view the media, which is owned and controlled by big business, wants to transport to the public in order to pursue the industries' interests. What does it count to have a critical statement by a foreign minister from Czech Republic or Poland, above all, new members who should not have too much of a say but simply be grateful for them being granted entry into the noble club as very arrogantly most German politicians pose it, if no western media reflects such thoughts or criticism? These media tools will certainly be employed for the ratification process of the "constitution" as one can expect the citizens to be very suspicious in regards to EU-beaurocracy. The leading classes in all EU countries has to fear that the constitution would either only get a very narrow majority in a public referendum in any of the member states or even be rejected as the Danish and Irish referenda in the past years showed. It took the Irish government a lot of efforts and a questionable trick to finally get their citizens to back the Nice-accord on expansion of the union and it's militarisation. Only because the Irish government was forced by their citizens who rejected the agreements of Nice in a first referendum to re-negotiate parts of the accord, mainly the passage of the European military rapid reaction force and "peacekeeping" missions were brought to the people again in a second referendum. Even after re-negotiating the Nice accord the government of Bertie Ahern had a hard time to win approval and relied on the influence of the catholic church whose priests and bishops campaigned in favour of the more than questionable agreement. In addition, the government saw reason to doubt the success of the second referendum and posed the question in a misleading style coming to the equivilant of "if you do not reject the Nice accord vote no". Funny enough, sociological studies on the German population show that the voters there would always tend to say "Yes" in a public survey or hypothetical referendum. In Ireland it is vice versa.

The German government under Schröder and Fischer rejects outright any demands for a people's referendum for a good reason: they know that the German people, if ever asked, would probably vote in their majority if not entirety "No". Although it has been Fischer's Green party which two decades ago entered the political arena on grounds of demanding a participating democracy governed by people's referenda they are now the first ones to reject such direct participation of the German people whereas even Social Democrats and Christian Conservatives seemed to be more receptive to this idea.

In other countries one can expect the same reluctance by the various governments. Especially in the new member states like Poland, Hungary and Czech Republic where the participation in the election to the European Parliament 13th June 2004 has been lower than in any existing member state it can be expected that the people won't accept the constitution. Since all governments and the EU Commission are aware of this reality they agreed on a ratification procedure which may lead to a very undemocratic ruling by the majority of member states over those states which have not ratified the closing act of the constitution within 2 years. In their declaration for the ratification the governments express their concern that the constitution could not be ratified in all member states and that in such a case "the European Council would convene in order to obtain a decision." This in very euphemistic terms shall suggest that a ratification could be enforced by a majority in the European

Council. Such a majority would overrule the will of the people of the relevant member states.

In order to make this possible the European Council has already been granted an unprecedented priviledge of self-imposing rules. In Article I-24 of the Constitution a so called "Passarelle" has been formulated allowing the European Council to change the rules from the requirement for unanimous voting to majority voting where deemed necessary. In other words, if one or more member states disagree in a certain matter with the others and do not give in to the pressure from the majority the majority may after a six months period decide to go ahead by a majority voting. The veto-like right of member states which has been a privilege since the EC's foundation has become useless under the terms of the new constitution.

3. The European Parliament—a paper-tiger?

While most Europeans might not feel any affiliation with the European Parliament and it's members whom the media in all member states does not grant a platform and for this reason let them appear anonymous, the development from 1979 when the parliament has been for the first time been voted on directly by the people in the member states of the European Community (EC), has been quite significant. Although the European Parliament is far from having fought for it's rights as the late chancellor of West Germany, Willy Brandt, himself a member of the European Parliament in 1979, had predicted, some acchievements have been made. When the European Union was founded in 1992, the Maastricht accord gave much more power to the EU Commission and the European Council, but not to the European Parliament. Nowadays, roughly 76% of all legal standards, rules and legislation are made in Bruxelles, but still the majority of the population of Europe shows no interest in European affairs. Maybe because it is too complex or appears to be inconcrete although the effects are felt by everybody. In such a situation the people should be interested in good representatives but the media creates a mystery around everything related to European. It is part of a misinformation campaign which shall divert anger from the national level to the "anonymous Brussels beaurocracy".

The new constitution won't make it much easier for parliamentarians to participate in the legislative process. Still, there won't be a right for the parliament to initiate legislation. If one regards EU Commission and European Council as the executive branch of the constitution the parliament has not much influence on these. Without this, the parliament will be a paper-tiger as it can only postulate that the EU Commission proposes legislation. Whether or not the Commission will do so will be subject to their own discretion. No wonder that the media does not pay a lot of attention to this parliament, and no wonder that the public remains sceptical.

All the European Parliament got from the Maastricht accord was in Article 251 the so called right to particpate. This clause also remains the same in the constitution's article III-302 which clearly states that the European Parliament has in key issues, such as the political fields of Foreign affairs and Security, Interior and Judicial matters as well as the Budget and Tax policy, only an advisory function. This is mocking any democratic principles which most of our nations have adhered to on a national level ever since the French Revolution in 1789.

4. Fischer for President...or Metternich versus Monnet

Another field where the European Parliament other than any national parliament has no influence is in the nomination of the future EU president. Still, the EU Commission president will be nominated by the national governments through the European Council. The only new aspect is that since the Nice accord (article 214 EGV) the European Parliament will be asked for its approval. The German government along with the governments of smaller countries pleaded for the election of a commission president by the European Parliament. Other countries, such as Greatbritain, Spain and France strongly refuted this as they probably feared that Germany accounting for the largest amount of MEP's would have the greatest influence and by this could push through their candidate who most likely will be foreign minister Joseph Fischer. Those countries preferred to have the EU government being formed by the European Council consisting of ministers from national governments. As the draft Constitution now defines the EU Commission president will be nominated by the European Council but voted on by the European Parliament. If a candidate does not receive the majority of votes the European Council within a month will nominate another candidate. This solution is closer to the British and French position than to the German. The idea to have a candidate only be nominated by the European Council and not the European Parliament or a fraction in it reflects the fear of the European governments that a direct election of the EU president through the parliament would probably lead to a politicisation of the EU commission. A president being nominated and voted on by parliament would be much more controllable through parliament rather than a puppet of the EU governments. The advocates for the present regulation that the president be nominated by the EU Council claim that the EU commission shall be neutral and not politicised. This may sound good, but the reality is that the EU commission never has been neutral but usually under tremendous pressure from the lobbyists of industries and banks. It would be good if the European parliament could become a counter-weight to the powerful EU commission and the European Council. A president being nominated and voted on by the parliament and not the governments themselves could certainly be much better be hold accountable for the EU commission's policy. By electing the EU president in parliament, politicisation of the commission would inevitably happen, but considering the power the commission has already, wouldn't it be a good idea? The bigger countries objected this method. Nevertheless it seems to be clear that after the Schröder government lost the 2006 Bundestag elections foreign minister Fischer, by his age not up for retirement yet, will be nominated the first EU president. As the initiative for legislation in the EU will be solely reserved for the EU commission and not the parliament it becomes obvious why the British, French and other nations were objecting to the Germanisation of the EU Commission. One can say that the British have not won the second worldwar for giving in to Frankfurt and Berlin, but in fact, as it stands, this is what will most likely happen.

5. Securing power by new voting mechanism...

In December 2000 the European Council at the Nice summit laid the grounds for the new voting regulations in the Council and by this strengthened the voting power of the larger states. France insisted on retaining 29 votes in the Council as Germany, Italy and Greatbritain each held 29 votes as well although these countries have a higher population. Poland and Spain each were granted 27 votes, a fact that proves that a political balance was sought as both populations together would not amount to what Germany does. On the other hand, the difference between Poland & Spain to France, Italy and Greatbritain is less than those three countries' difference to Germany. The unbalance resulted from the fact that in Nice four countries were given the same amount, 29 votes, although Germany accounted for a much higher population. For the first time ever in the history of the EU legislation can be brought down by a veto if not at least 62% of the population of the EU are represented. This veto can only be used to block legislation, it is not a quorum to initiate same. In reality this means that only Germany will benefit from the population quorum based veto as it would only need to find one ally among the larger states and let's say a smaller state like Luxembourg and could block all EU legislation by throwing in the population joker card. Germany could also block decisions by winning the support of two of the three next smaller states. All other large states would need for this at least three partners. Therefore, effectively only Germany benefits from the new voting regulations. We can well imagine how the German government will lobby the Polish government by reminding the Polish of the German industries' investment into Poland and their dependencies on the German industries and by this win the Polish governments' support against a legislation the German government, or better: the German industry does not want to become effective. The underrepresentation in the council by weighing the 29 votes Germany has likewise France, Italy and Greatbritain becomes irrelevant when Germany trhows in it's population quorum. Article 1-24 of the new constitution now proclaims that this voting mechanism becomes a mandatory requirement for any decision which calls for a qualified majority. If, i.e. the European Council decides over far reaching initiatives it has to have the majority of member states as well as three Fifth of the EU's population back up the decision. Assumed that the EU soon counts 25 member states up to 12 could be defeated in a vote while the citizens effected would be 180 million of the 450 million. What will change with the new constitution? Presently, in a Union of 25 member states one needs at least 72.3% of the votes in the Council, a majority of the member states as well as the back-up by states representing 62% of the population. If the population quorum becomes the relevant requirement the balance of power between the member states would shift dramatically towards the four largest members, Germany, Greatbritain, France and Italy of which Germany as the most populous one would benefit most. As these four countries currently each hold 29 votes of the 345 total votes after expansion to 25 members they would each account for only 8.4%. With the population quorum becoming relevant the influence of Germany would double and now be 17% while France, Greatbritain and Italy would only make it to 12% each. Spain and Poland would only gain 0.2%, from 7.8 % to 8%. Their influence becomes significantly smaller which may explain their fierce resistance against the new constitution. If one considers the potential constellations in the Council, one can clearly see that the four countries, Germany, Greatbritain, France and Italy already account for 53% of the requires 60% which are needed for a quqlified majority. In order to pass a decision with qualified majority one also needs the majority of member states. In this regard the smaller countries have the same vote as the larger ones. The larger countries will be free to find partners and thus the smaller countries may bec ome crucial. Loosers in this would be countries of the middle field, such as Poland, Spaain, The Netherlands, but also countries with roughly 10 million inhabitants, such as Belgium, Greece, Portugal, Hungary and Czech Republic. By introducing the demographic factor for decision making their influence becomes almost irrelevant and their importance as a partner for the bigger states is shrinking. If one sees both voting systems, the Nice accord as well as the new system spon-sored by the new constitution and considers that the 15 members of the old EU would under present voting regulations in the new EU of 25 states could barely hold a thin majority. If Bulgaria and Romania are to join, so that the EU counts 27 members, the old EU members would loose their majority. How interesting could it be to see the exist-ing EU members being outnumbered by the new members! Imagine, founding states like France, Germany, Italy and Greatbritain would be told by countries like Poland, Bulgaria, Romania, Lithuania what they think is right! To prevent this from happening the key states of today's EU have made sure that they will always have things under control. Under their control. And Germany plays the most important role in this priviledged club, otherwise, I believe, they would never ever have agreed to it.

6. Militarisation and Neoliberal Agenda

There has been much talk about the new constitution. What is it we as ordinary citizens have to fear? Will the EU be turned into a regime like the United States of America after 11th September 2001? Will we see the rise of a dictatorship? Will NAZIS rule over Europe? I think we can exclude all these scenarios. What is striking me is the fact that every-thing happening at present seems to go unnoticed and unreflected while those fellow Europeans who think about it seem to feel power-less, even paralysed. This could be a strategy by the ruling class in

Europe. As outlined before, it is easy for local or national politicians to blame Bruxelles, an anonymous beauraucracy noone trusts. Because the transforming process of the EU happens almost overnight and unnoticed by the public it happens smoothly. Many fellow Europeans also seem to have no problem with the militarisation of the EU as they sense that ultimately it could be important to have military might in case one is confronted with a threat which could very well be coming from the US. On the other hand, many of the EU citizens do not see that while it is probably right that there is rivalry between the US and the EU that the EU is adopting more from the US than many of us would ever have believed. I am not talking of the life style of the US. The eating habbits and cultural acchievements which many of the younger Europeans nowadays criticise. No, I speak of the economic agenda. The Hire & Fire System, the pure profit maximisation and shareholder value philosophy we in the EU have not only copied so far quite well, but are to perfectionise. This is the real threat I see for our society but I also see that as long as we do not interfere with the US American interests we won't have any problems with them. So why would it become necessary that the EU is arming itself? If we are Capitalists both sides of the atlantic, why would we need to deter eachother? Or could it be that 60 years after the end of WWII again German (this time European, but then again, the Central Bank is in Frankfurt) capital stands against American capital. If the German EU becomes as powerful as the Third Reich thought it was, we might see tensions across the atlantic. Given the fact that the world economy is in a crisis worse than in 1929 one might think we are doing good to arm ourselves. The only problem is that arms do not make this planet a safer place. And I would rather like to see the EU's weapons be not used but used as a deterrent against anybody to attack us if the economic foundation our federation is laid on would be not neoliberal but progressive. I would not have a problem to know that the force de frappe, the French nukes, protect a more social and liberal system against a clearly capitalistic and imperialistic system but the reality seems to be that we are turning Europe economical into a copy of US America and would only defend our capitalistic society against theirs. That can never be a good outcome but only a world war destroying everything.

In other words, as long as I don't see any fundamental change in our economic policy towards a more social, fair and just system, I would rather see us not have any weapons at all as there would be nothing to defend which we could not have if we joined the US as their 52nd state.

Militarisation of EU foreign policy

The proposed constitution calls for the member states to "gradually improve their military abilities". Article I-40 makes it obligatory for the members of the EU to buy more and more weapons, even those we once were told had to be taken away from a man like Saddam Hussein because they were too dangerous. We, the European Union, will, of course, only buy those chemical, biological and nuclear weapons in order not to use them. A few bags of cement would do but we were told that we might have to use these in case we are attacked.

Article III-212 of the Constitution goes even further. It calls for an "European Institution for Armament, Military Science and Improvement of Military Abilities". Until now the defence budgets have been varying a lot from 0.75% of the GDP in Ireland to 1.5% in Germany, 2.5% in France, 2.7% in Greatbritain and unbelievable 4.91 % in Greece. The US nowadays spends 3.03% of it's GDP for arms. In absolute figures all 15 EU states spend 170 billion € whereas the US in 2003 spent 285 billion €. Both blocks pledged to drastically increase their defence budgets over the coming years. With the creation of the European Agency for Armament the control of the arms race will be out of the reach of the EU parliament or even the European Court of Justice, not to speak of national parliaments which until the new onstitution will become effective always had a say in this aspect. According to the constitution's Article III-205 the European parliament will only have the right to be notified and consulted in this regard. It will only be the EU council, the governments of the member states so to speak, which will have power over the budget and the Agency for Armament according to Article III-207. Not even the Bush regime in the US has the sole power over how much the oil industry wants to spend on their adventures in the Middle East. Another frightening fact is that the new constitution calls for a steady increase of the defence budget while it is clear that the military-industrial complex of Germany, France, Great-britain and Italy, especially the Airbus conglomerate will benefit from this giving Bush a reason to verbally attack this development and citing illegal contributions by governments. Bush was leashing out against Airbus and the fact that by government subsidies of EU member states an unfair competition advantage was granted to the passenger planes of Airbus which threaten Boeing. This itself is hipocritical as the US government clearly sponsors their military-industrial complex during their "War on Terror". A significant amount of the US' defence budget goes directly to Boeing which not only builds passenger planes.

Not only are the strategic consequences of an arms race and military rivalry with the US dangerous and unhealthy for world peace but someone simply has to pay for it and we can well imagine who it will be: the taxpayer in all member states. At the same time the ruling class as well as their political establishment and media never get tired to tell us that not the impertinant theft of the state's money by the multinational corporations and their shareholders by means of the neoliberal tax reforms implied are responsible for the empty pockets of the state but the exploding social expenditure, which is, of course, a lie. The neoliberal logic of Schröder, Blair and Berlusconi demands that tax payer's money is pumped into armament. For this, we unfortunately still have funds.

Uncontrolled policing and prosecution

In the interior politics one can observe an unprecedented radicalisation towards a policing state. By employing the best excuse we will have in this century, the so called "9/11—excuse" Europe's hardliners were able to push through legislation turning the member states into policing states. Like in the case of the foreign and security policy the events of 11th September 2001 had a catalyzing effect, meaning that no doubts are allowed anymore when we ordinary citizens question the tough regime in these areas. Our mouths will be shut by a harsh "haven't you watched tv, didn't you see the collapsing skyscrapers? Don't you want that we protect ourselves?". And anyone who questions the necessity for a tight security regime could be seen as someone sympathising with terrorists or being a terrorrist himself. There seems to be no room for any rational thinking. Although governments and parliaments have a responsibility not to make ad hoc decisions over longterm commitments for legislation the Constitution will reflect to a large degree that the convent members were influenced by 9/11. The closing statement of the convent task group for interior and judicial policy openly admits that "the attacks of 11th September have lead to some immediate regulations such as the creation of an European arrest warrant and the coordination of the operational cooperation in fighting criminality as well as terrorism and surveillence of the EU's outside borders".

What bothers me is not the fact that our states cooperate and exchange data on terrorists and by this may have at least a chance to prevent attacks, but the fact that these new agencies like Eurojust, a institution for judicial cooperation, and a soon to be founded European Public Prosecutor's office are not controlled by the EU parliament which again is only granted an advisory status until now. We have already seen that EUROPOL could not be controlled and managed well by the EU as the police forces sent to Europol are employed under their national law and can only be held accountablee in their member states. On the other hand Article III-177 construes that Europol and Eurojust shall work under one roof and have wide ranging authorities throughout the European Union. It is frightening to imagine that a police shall get a so much power and that the people working for this force can not be held responsible by any European institution but only by national governments and con trolled through national parliaments. In the constitution's article III-177/2 provision is made for control by European as well as national parliaments but no definition of the rights to control are made. Everything remains more than vague, for a good reason as one can rfead in the protocol of the task group: "It has not been our task to define the authorities of Europol but to leave room for the legislators to expand these authorities." So there is no constitutional limit to the policing authorities of Europol. In all our states we have more or less strict and accurate laws describing what police could and should do with providing clear definitions and limitations in order to protect the citizens from abuse of power and corruption.

The same applies to the creation of a European Public Prosecutor's office which according to Article III-175 may have the authority to prosecute criminals throughout the European Union again without any controlling method by courts or the EU parliament. Although many members in the convent task group remained highly skeptical against such a mega prosecution potential German foreign minister Joseph Fischer pushed through this agenda vigorously argueing that transnational criminals and terrorists may exploit the situation if the EU had no such public prosecutor's office as if the member states so far had no police, state prosecutors and judges.

As no control function is granted to either the European Court of Justic nor to the European Parliament one can imagine that if the ruling class in Europe feels threatened by political movements they may use these new policing institutions as a tool for surpression. An uncontrolled police and prosecution agency is what we Germans have painful experience with, in both regimes last century. The Gestapo of the Third Reich has been uncontrolled and became the death squad against political opponents. Although on a very different scale the surpressive tools of the East German STASI taught us a lesson that millions of files used against the citizens of a state do not prevent it from disappearing. Therefore, with the creation of prosecution and policing agencies lacking any democratically controlled counterweight our civil rights are at stake.

Another terrifying attack against our freedom has been launched by the "task group article 36" which shall become the coordination gremium of the Council dealing with everything which usually a Ministry of the Interior would cover, i.e. policing, judicial matters, civil protection as well as customs and immigration. So, although the constitution does not expressly prrovide for the creation of a European Ministry of the Interior, this gremium of civil servants will direct from Bruxelles the security matters, policing and protection of the outer borders of the EU and by this become de-facto a Ministry of the Interior supervising any kind of execution of state power throughout the union. This gremium may be installed by the European Council without any controlling power given to the European Parliament. There is also no provision for any control through the courts, like i.e. the European Court of Justice. No, this gremium will receive it's orders directly from the Council which will have the priviledge to legislate the body which it solely controles and by this become as in many other issues the legislative and executive branch. The traditional division of power as a principal of our so called Western democracies has been burried almost unnoticed.

Economic strategy

The economic agenda of the European Union will be as neoliberal as the Maastricht accord in the early nineties defined "economic stability" as a fiscal austerity that forced those countries adopting the EURO to commit to a crackdown on social, cultural and ecological standards. As if our political leaders haven't learnt a lesson from the 1990ies during which the virtual reality casino of the stock markets, new technology "boom" and fraudulant financial markets created an incredible unemployment as well as a new gulf between rich and poor leading us into a crisis as serious as between the two world wars, they try to let this neoliberal appear to be ineviatble and without alternative. In the new constitution's article III-69 they subscribe to an "unrestricted free market governed by competition" which abides to the principles laid by the governmental conference in June 2004. These principles describe the "Growth & Stability Pact" and the contained price stability as the ultima ratio. In Article I-3 the "Cultural diversity as well as arts" will be reduced to a minimum, just in line with the WTO regulations (III-55). The fight against unemployment will be subordinated to the overall economic policy (III-100) and governed by the one-sided orientation of the European Central Bank on their principle of price stability (Article I-29) as well as the "Stability Pact" (Art. III-76). Another crucial aspect is taxation. Only the indirect taxes, such as VAT, Petrol-, Alcohol, Luxury-Goods Tax etc. shall be harmonised but not the income and corporate taxes. Therefore, the ruining process of tax dumping will be inforced. Major coporations will follow the mere logic of investing only in countries of dwindling tax rates. Member states continue to compete with eachother in lowering corporate taxes and in the end no taxes will be paid by those rich multinational corporations and stock market listed companies who often received structural funds and subsidies from Bruxelles, our tax payers pay and by this encourage those beneficiaries to further cut down employment as well as labour-, social- as well as ecological standards. Thus, the EU Constitution is falling back well behind what our West German constitution, the Basic Law, still holds up as a key goal: a socially balanced free market with no exclusions of public ownership where beneficial or necessary. This has been for four decades the success model of West Germany guaranteeing social rights *and* free entrepreneurship, all relatively well balanced. It will be difficult to explain to the German people why this has to be given up now, especially since the desastrous consequences of an unregulated Manchester Capitalism becomes more and more obvious. But not only the West Germans will miss their relatively liberal and human rights focused Basic Law but also East Germans who traditionally enjoyed much more social rights until unification. In their eyes the so called western democracies and their economic system may further loose credibility and acceptance.

7. European Expansion—Tabula Rasa in Eastern Europe

While we heard a lot of the so called East-West divide in Europe finally to be overcome and East European countries being brought back into the family of Western democracies the financial daily Handelsblatt[3] concentrated in the for their readers important question how these can maximise the profit of their inherited or somehow collected millions and billions. The news that the expansion of the EU towards the east will create the biggest profits in the German portfolios certainly encouraged Germany's shareholders to invest in DAX listed corporations rather than in EUROSTOXX 50 multinational companies. The reason for this: the Eurostoxx listed companies are expecting a growth in return on investment by 17% while the DAX listed coporations are probably gaining 50% or more after they accumulated 30% in the year before (2003). This incredible growth will only partly be owed to the crack down on the social system and everything Schröder calls "painful but necessary reforms" but also to the expansion towards the East. As Germany's industry had been suffering from an expansion crisis the collaps of the trade barriers will particularily be beneficial to the DAX listed German retailers as well as financial institutions and car manufacturers. On the one hand the expectations are high in terms of consumption but on the other hand also for reducing production costs due to labour costs which are in many cases only a fraction of those of Germany or any other West European countries. An hour of labor in Lithuania for instance costs only 2.42 €, in Estonia 3.03 €, in Poland 4.48 €, in Slovenia 8.98 € including social costs. Compared to West European costs of roughly 20 € per hour it will be a great field for speculation and profit maximisation. Not only will this lead to a job

---

3.   Handelsblatt 29th March 2004 "DAX Titel profitieren von Ost-Erweiterung"

transfer towards to the East and by this let unemployment in the "old" EU hit the ceiling but also to the collaps of medium sized companies in the East which can not compete with the wholesalers and major production companies from the West. Also, many farmers in the new member states will be ruined as they can't compete with the highly subsidised agricultural sector of the West European countries. And it had been made crystal clear to Poland that they won't get the same financial support for their farmers like the Irish, French, Austrian and other "old" members for decades got. Moreover, the West German retailers will not only open their supermarket chains in the East but also provide the products, a situation we have already observed when the GDR was taken over by West Germany in 1990.

In contrast to the hostile take-over in 1990 we can say that this process is already well under way since several years when East European state holdings were privatised and in many cases sold to West European "investors". In the financial sector of Poland and Czech Republic one can say that more than 70% of the banks are now owned by the West European banks, in Hungary 60% and in Slovakia 80%. German wholesaler Metro and car manufacturers like VW are aggressively gaining significant market shares.

But the EU expansion not only means that West European companies and shareholders are benefitting from profit maximisation but also receive the bulk of the EU subsidies paid to the new member states. This leads to the perverse situation that the taxpayers in West European countries finance the transfer of jobs to the East while in the new member states the medium sized manufacturers and retailers will be ruined. The only ones to gain from this blunt and deliberate fraud are the West European major corporations, especially those listed in the DAX. The labour costs and wages in West European countries as a consequence will further be under pressure and therefore will shrink to a minimum. In the East European countries we won't see a rise in income and wealth but in the number of EU subsidised cheap labour and also unemployment and social desaster as due to the steadily decreasing corporate taxes the state's pockets will be empty in those countries as well. In other words, the same development can be foreseen as in Germany after Schröder's tax-reform. It is ridiculous in this regard that the mega tax-dumper now criticises the new tax-dumpers in Eastern Europe but that's why Schröder has been labeled Europe's leading reformist. The hipocracy is unrivaled. A European tax harmonisation could have been agreed on but one never heard Schröder even suggest such initiative to prevent a tax dumping competition among the member countries. One could have agreed on a minimum corporate tax rate across Europe rather than the unhealthy Maastricht "stability" pact. "Everybody as an average becomes richer", concludes the Handelsblatt in it's editorial. That will be true. On an average basis always everybody will be richer but the same one could say about the world economy. For some reason "on an average basis" does not mean that the majority does not get poorer while the top ten thousand shareholders on this planet become richer and richer, especially after the new EU members have been "allowed" entry into the noble club of the EU.

7

Germany's Domestic Agenda

1. Germany in Crisis shifts to the Right

Wit the election of former IMF boss Horst Köhler into the country's highest position as Federal President, Germany's industrial leadership and political class indicated that the traditionally ceremonial office of president will become the centre of a movement towards the right. Köhler, whom I interviewed when he was heading the IMF and in this function paid a visit to Argentina weeks after President Kirchner took the oth of office in Spring 2003, is known as a brutal neo-liberal economist who has the benefit not to have any diplomatic talent. During the interview he stressed that ownership rights as well as "free market" principles should have priority over any government decision, even in a troublesome spot like Argentina which because of the neo-liberal exploitation in the Menem-years has piled-up billions over billions of foreign debt. My question how he could justify the strict IMF policy in a case like Argentina where people were almost starving following the desastrous Dollar-Peso parity which only benefitted the rich class and the international banks was answered by Köhler by saying that off course one needs to evaluate a situation but that in the end debts had to be paid, no matter what. And one could see how much the government of President Kirchner strugggled in the due course when trying to find a solution in delaing with the foreign banks. Köhler has in this case not been of any help. When he was nominated by the Christian Democratic Union to become Germany's president he made clear that he would not revert to the traditionally ceremonial part of the office but wouldd intervene whereever he feels it is necessary. As usual, the media applauds even before one has a clear idea about what this president will focus on. In a way, one could say, we can expect another shift to the right with a banker to be our president now. It must be a logic development of neo-liberalism that a banker shall play the role of a moral institution.

"Germany is still in a crisis" assert the leading economists in their statement in the summer of 2004. The production of goods in the first half of 2004 has further decreased, especially consumer goods showed a drastic decline of 5.5% but also the number of longterm investment goods fell back by 1.2%. The construction business stagnates, medium sized retailers are still on death row and the overrall business climate in Germany is worse than ever in the past 30 years. The daily "Handelsblatt" titled "Consumers on Strike" and note that the consumers do not only not spend money as they used to but also seem to be unwilling to put it onto their savings accounts or invest it into funds. It's easy to blame the evil ordinary consumers who are simply unwilling to spend their money and give the economy a boost. The idea that the ordinary consumers don't have any more money to spend sounds not too far fetched but nevertheless it is not reflected by the German media. In reality, most people nowadays have to either cut their savings or even supply their daily living expenses with cash from their savings accounts. On the other hand, why should those top ten per cent of our society fill their villas and carports with all these vcr, tvs, washing machines, middle class cars? They won't buy more even if Schröder's tax reform makes them richer and richer. They got everything, so they won't close the gap the ordinary consumers are responsible for. The truth is that most consumers cut down on consumption not because they don't want to buy a new car, washing machine or tv, but simply cut down on those investments which are not absolutely necessary. They also spend less money on travel or other holidays while a growing number does not have vacations any more at all although they got enough time for such.

The socialistic system promised that we would get everything we needed. Capitalism promises that we will need everything we will get. Somehow this promise can not be lived up to under capitalistic rules as people would certainly want to work and earn a good salary they would love to spend for luxury goods but first of all the shrinking wages which are in most areas nowadays lower than in 1980 (clear of inflation) and secondly a dramatically increasing unemployment along with drastically reduced redundancy payments and a torpedoed social system are the true factors being responsible for the current consumer abstantion.

I bet that those people who will fall under the new regulations of a labour market reform referred to as "Hartz IV" which shall force unemployees to pick up any kind of job no matter what qualification they may have and no matter how badly paid (usually well below the minimum wages once agreed upon between unions and corporations) these jobs are, won't be those people who will ignite the next economic boom by increasing the domestic demand.

Seen at daylight Neoliberalism has the charme of a therapy pretending to bring a starving person back on his own feet by cutting down on his diet and which cites any collaps of the poor fellow as an indication that the supply with calories was still to high and in the interest of recovery needs to be further cut down. But one should not forget that the starving person is not put on minimalistic diet because of incompentency of his doctors to draw the right conclusions from their diagnose but because there are other people who will increase their standard of living by exactly what he has been denied. While the unions are already accused for their modest demand of 3% pay increase after years of abstantion as being ignorant to the economic crisis the 30 DAX listed major corporations increase their share dividend paid out to shareholders by 6% in 2004 as their profit margins have risen by more than 30% in 2003.[1]

Especially Deutsche Bank AG was able to increase it's profit from 397 million Euros in 2002 to incredible 1.37 billion Euros in 2003 while the official result as per their balance sheet in 2003 increased by 163% to 3.6 billion Euros, this effect partly owed to Schröder's tax reform.[2] And another major corporation who always publically moans about high labour costs, Daimler-Chrysler, has managed to aggregate 5.1 billion Euros in profit while the overall balance suggests a decrease in production worth 136.4 billion Euros. And, like in the US, the energy consortiums are the real winners of this development. Eon and RWE will increase their dividend in 2004 by 14% as their profits rose by 67% (Eon) and 23% (RWE) in 2003.[3]

Give the fact that these mega corporations had once been held by the state and have only been privatised in recent years one may ask the question why the state would give away such lucrative businesses who by several mergers have become a duopoli controling the energy market and by this the prices if corruption has not played a role. Together, and that's where the profit of these giants come from, they decide to increase the tariffs at their sole deiscretion and with immediate consequences for us consumers whether we are rich or poor. As there is no competition in the market and lacking any alternative we are directly financing their shareholder's profit. Another reason, why the consumers can not increase domestic demand.

If one doesn't want to sit in a dark, cold apartement one has to pay whether or not one is unemployed, a pensioneer or still in the possession of a well paid job. In this aspect a delicate effect of the "Red-Green"—government's "ecologically sound tax reform" (Yeah, that's what Schröder & Fischer called it!) can be observed in the increase of taxes on energy hitting those who had been robbed of their social exist-

1.   Handelsblatt 29th March 2004 "DAX Konzerne zahlen mehr Dividende"
2.   Handelsblatt 6th February 2004 "Deutsche Bank hat 2003 Ertragswende geschafft"
3.   Handelsblatt 11th March 2004 "Deutscher Energiemarkt legt zu"

ence as anybody else but with a much more tragic effect, while said tax reform granted tax exempts for 23 industrial areas which are relying on energy heavily. This shows how "social" Schröder's SPD and how "ecological" Fischer's Green Party really are.

The deregulation and privatisation movement has not increased the productivity of our economies or have them even become more con-sumer-friendly as it has always been promised by the neoliberals but made the major European corporations and their owners richer, the banks bigger, more powerful and also richer while hundreds of thou-sands of jobs were killed. The liberalisation of the postal services in Europe between 1990 and 2001 laid off 130,000 postal workers and forced millions of others to work for less and without social benefits as it had been said that this would increase efficiency although I can not see any logic in the fact that post offices and letter boxes which can be reached by everyone even by foot has been inefficient. Likewise has the liberalisation of the European electricity and gas markets during the second half of the nineties lead to a lay-off in the reagion of 80,000 employees, more than a quarter of the workforce in this field in 1995. At the same time the energy prices increased significantly.

Also, the privatisation of the German railway, the good old Bundes-bahn, presently known as Deutsche Bahn AG, has not lead to more competitive ticket prices and better service but in the contrary to a reduced service and a widespreading cut in tracks being served throughout the country. It is true, the service of the state-owned Bundesbahn had been inflexible and oldfashioned, but today the ser-vice of the privatised Deutsche Bahn AG is not more flexible and not more attractive but less. I understand that there have been routes which have not been economically viable but a public service like trans-portation has to be seen under different but only economic aspects. We can not demand from our people to become more flexible and accept job offers requiring travel if we do not provide the necessary transport. And we can not pledge to be driven by environmental thinking while cutting down on public transport forcing people to either use a car, or if they are unemployed or old and have none, stay at home. This is neither fair nor economically wise. Therefore, the railway services probably can not be managed under the profitability rules of the stock markets, especially not when safety is at stake as the British railway system has prooven tragically. Now, the British Railtrack is more or less under government control again.

Although it has become clear with above examples that in certain areas of public life or essential public services such as universities, hospitals, senior citizen residents, libraries, transportation, energy and vital resources private ownership is counterproductive and only benefits the rich classes our politicians continue to axe what they and their lobbying friends consider not efficient. Anyone who is now advocating the further privatisation of our health care system should have a look across the Atlantic where today 41 million US-Americans do not even have cover for health and where the personal income directly decides over someones' life expectancy. And a privatised health care system is not even less costly as the US-American example shows since the US account for the highest per capita—spending although 41 million Americans do not benefit from that. As always the rich and most of the middle class are able to afford the private health insurance and pension plans but what about those who have been neglected their right to work, or those who suffer from inabilities or a old? Under the present "Social Democratic & Green" government the US model is copied as if it has been a success. Of course, the Green Party today is a very different party from what it has been when it was founded by environmentalists and pacisfists in the 1980ies but since then it underwent a significant change. Its' clientele today consists of what Fischer once stood against: the establishment. Those how are well-off today used to be in universities and many of them in studen and peace movements in the sixties and seventies. A recent study published by Spiegel magazine revealed that not the liberals of the FDP are nowadays considered the party of the better-off but the Greens. Those who once screamed "Ho-

Chi-Minh" when demonstrating on West-Berlin's Ku'damm and have been knocked down by water canons are now defending their privileges along with their multi-cultural attitude which in numerous cases serves only as an excuse for not being nationalistic or even chauvenistic. Well, from the Greens one would not expect to be more social or even socialistic as they never had their roots in any ideology or philosophy, but from the "Social Democrats" one should have expected a great deal of solidarity, especially when seen under the light of history, as it has been Social Democrats who formed resistance against Bismarck and won certain social rights.

It is also questionable why "Social Democrats" who once fought for equal access to education are eager to introduce a system of so called "Elite Universities" modeled on the US system when one can see how proud some of these reputable institutions are to once have enrolled such an outstanding student as George W. Bush as long as his dad payed. Germany will soon have a Daimler-Chrysler University residing in the former seat of the Honecker-government in East Berlin. The building today belongs to the City of Berlin and could be used for public or at least be rented out to said institution for sons and daughters of Germany's "elite" but the city government of SPD and reform socialist PDS has the guts to give it away for nothing while at the same time cutting down on free text books for Berlin's elementary and secondary schools.

The symptoms described above are quite similar across Europe. None of the European countries abiding to the already 14 year-long lasting neoliberal agenda has enjoyed prosperity and growth but is torn by the highest unemployment, slowest economic growth and greatest poverty with the life-situation of the great majority of Europeans being at vere greater risk since the end of World War II. We are being told by the media and our ruling class of politicians and sometimes by even those who are now in opposition that there is no alternative to "Globalisation" and Capitalism as our state has less and less money to spend and because our social system had expanded too much. We are told by the media that we are eating up our granny's house and are leaving tremendous debts behind which our children and grandchildren would feel as a heavy burden. Indeed, public funds are quite restricted these days. Most communities and cities in Germany are facing bankruptcy these days, especially since Schröder's tax reform became effective. Presently every fifth Euro received from taxpayers is used to pay interest to the banks without even paying back the principals of these loans. One has to quesxtion of course the legitimacy of those debts. It has been the Social Democratic—Liberal government of Chancellor Helmut Schmidt who increased the debt as West—Germany's industry at that time was in a classical expansion crisis. The artificially created Oil Crisis of 1979/1980 could have been averted by the government by subsidizing fuel bas little as maybe 5 billion Deutsche Marks at that time but the West-German captains of industry told Chancellor Schmidt clearly that they "needed" the second oil crisis in order to gain credibility for their first attack on the social system. West-Germans very well remembered the oil crisis of 1974 and understood that cuts had to be made. It sounded so logic. Yes, the economy was in a malaise because of the high oil prices, everyone could follow this train of thought. And Chancellor Schmidt made an effort to explain to us that painful decisions had to be made. Those decision being imposed on him, of course. Nobody could question this as everyone saw in the news that the oil prices really were higher than usual. The Social Democratic/Liberal government probably did what they could in order to avoid too drastic social cuts. That's why the West-German industry decided that Helmut Schmidt was not the right man to push through their demands to cut down the social welfare state. Not that he was not willing to. He started already what his successor as chancellor, Helmut Kohl, later did for 16 years. But Schmidt still tried to level out the system and increased the state's debt. This, of course, was not exactly what the captains of West-German industry wanted and Schmidt, a Social Democrat, still listend too much for their taste to the unions and his party's leftist fraction. That's why they replaced Schmidt with Kohl. The first names were the same anyway.

The irony is that today Germany's government bonds, the so called "Schatzbriefe" or treasuary bonds, are held by those institutional "investors", banks and privateers who forced the state deeper and deeper into debt by avoiding and evading taxes, economic blackmailing and their well-known lobbyism. And because the German state feels grateful to those rich banks and owners of it's industry we, the taxpayers, honour this impertinent theft by paying interest from money we would desperately need to finance public healthcare, pensions, schools, universities, libraries, cultural- and sport events. It is ridiculous but unfortunately it is not a joke.

Today, we are still confronted with the neoliberal mantra that our social system had expanded too much and could not be financed anymore. But is this really true? What is irritating is the fact that per capita the German industry produces today three times of what it produced in 1960. In the last ten years alone the real income of all of Germany increased by stunning 16%. Statistically, we are all rich. We Germans own three thousand billions of Euros, 150,000 Euros per nose. Unfortunately, not all of us own our own noses.

It is clear that one can accumulate money from money. While the wages stagnated since the nineties and even decline for many of us the income from property and ownership rights since 1990 has increased by 60%. Despite economic crisis and mass lay-offs 14 of the DAX listed major coporations have increased their shareholder value this year while the unions are already portrayed as impertinent the increase in the profit of the DAX listed corporations in 2003 has risen by 30%. The believers in neoliberalism, of course, always maintain that the profit would be re-invested and by this secure jobs. This is a blatant lie. If it was true, they would not increase the shareholder value while laying off workforce on an unprecedented scale. So lack of funds can not be the real reason for our state being almost bankrupt. Also, it can not be an expanding social spending as the media wants to make us believe. It has always been a legend easy to adhere to that social welfare, health care costs and pensions "exploded". In reality the social expenditure of Germany over the past 30 years has always been the same. In 1975 it accounted for 34% of the GDP, in 1994 for 33.3% and since 1997 again at 34.4% of the nation's GDP. The truth is that behind those figures one can see a dramatic cut-down on social expenditure as unemployment doubled within the past 30 years. With the growing number of unemployees the amount of people who have to finance their existance through public funds has increased but not the spending. These people are certainly not those who live a life in luxury as it is always said by the media in our country. Instead, there are others to which the state takes a generous approach. Under the Red/Green government Germany has become a tax haven for major coprorations and rich privateers. They pay almost no taxes at all anymore while the employees are accounting for the double share in the overall taxes collected compared with the share of those corporations. Thirty years ago it has been the other way around. After abolishing the property & wealth tax in 1996 by Chancellor Helmut Kohl the new government of Gerhard Schröder having pledged in their election campaign to reintroduce this tax which until 1996 swept annually 9 billion Deutsche Mark into the state's pockets abstained from this as well. This tax had only been paid by the richest families in our country. By not charging this minimal tax the state has since 1997 lost already 50 billion Euros. Another breakthrough for the Schröder-tax dumping has been the reduction of the corporate taxes to 25% while corporations, and we only talk about the richest ones again, were able to compensate the higher taxes they previously paid with the lower taxes after the reform. In 2000 it has still been 23 billion Euros what the state got from this tax, in 2001 it became negative (-0.4 billion €) and today it is zero. The most impertinent theft orchestrated by Schröder and his gang has been the abolishment of the taxes for selling holding companies. Deutsche Bank AG in 2002 gained one billion Euros when selling their shares held in Münchener Rück and Allianz AG. The centrepiece of the Schröd tax reform has been the income tax. Well, Schröder calling himself a "Social Democrat" had to hand out a few candies for his party's traditional clientele. An employee, married, no kids, earning 20,000 € per annum will save 1.168 € in income taxes. A top manager, married, no kids, earning one Million Euros per annum will save 102.453 €, or in other words, Schröder will give a Mercedes S class or BMW 5er limousine for free to those income-millioneers. At the same time Schröder cracks down on social welfare, unemployment benefits and pensions, citing the necessity to "save" funds for the state.

If asked, ministers of the Schröder-Fischer government repeat their mantra that taxes are too high and international competition too strong and that they only do what they have to do in order to save jobs in Germany. That's another lie. Germany has, in relation to its GNP, the second lowest tax quote (21.7%) compared with all OECD member states, following Japan. Even the US' tax quote is higher (22.7%), France 28.9% and Greatbritain 31%. The ordinary tax payer in Germany does not feel this.

In 1980 the taxes imposed on employees amounted to 28.7% while profits were taxed at 22.1%, in 1998 an average of 35.4% on the payroll and only 8.6% on profits. The taxes on property account for only 0.9% of the GNP while in the US it is 3.1%, in France 3.2% and in Greatbritain 3.9%. The corporate tax in Germany nominally is 25% but the real burden lying on the factor capital is much lower. The EU Commission calculated that the corporate taxes, levy, and property taxes all together in Germany amount to 22.6%, the second lowest level in the EU after Greece. The average throughout the EU is 29.8% while labour is taxed in Germany at 39.9% (37% EU average). Germany could and should fight against tax dumping by advocating a common level within the EU. It would be wise not to fight for the lowest level but a reasonable one which keeps the public services, social system as well as companies afloat. It would be possible but I fear that our leaders don't want this.

2. Armament

The federal budget for 2001 remained steady although the economy has been in recession. While the social budget is continously melting, the defense budget grew by 3.2 per cent to 46.8 billion DM (roughly 22 billion EUR) but it wasn't only Germany's own defense budget that grew. Export of weapons made Germany the fourth-largest weapons exporter after U.S., France and Russia.[4]

Especially, the Red-Green coalition government almost doubled weapons exports by giving approval for more than 2000 shipments, and by this raising the figure from 3.1 billion EUR to 4.6 billion EUR, most of it to Spain, Israel, Indonesia and Turkey, except for the first one, all crisis areas.[5] Quite astonishing, if one remembers that it was the Green party who always played the pacifist's songs and the Social Democrats who said it was unbearable for them to imagine that weapons are delivered with the blessing of the government (at that time the Kohl government) to Turkey, and that one can not exclude that with these weapons women and children are murdered, as former Defense Minister Rudolf Scharping asserted before he and Schröder assumed power. Within a year after Schröder-Fischer took over from Kohl, German weapons exports rose from 1.3 billion Deutsche Mark in 1998 to 2.8 billion Deutsche Mark in 1999.[6]

When the German Bundestag passed legislation to commit 3900 soldiers to the "war against terrorism" on 16th November, 2001, the defense budget also increased from 46.2 billion DM to 47.7 billion DM (23.5 Billion EUR). In July, 2002, Opel, the speaker for defense policy of the Social Democrats, pledged an easing of strict export control laws for weapons. He said, "when it comes to weapons export we follow an ideology which simply is contraproductive".[7] Germany is living on exports, and this should also apply to weapons, he said.

---

4.   Frankfurter Allgemeine Zeitung (FAZ) 27th October 1999
5.   Berliner Zeitung 24th November 2001
6.   Westfälischer Anzeiger Hamm 23rd October 2001
7.   Handelsblatt 12th July 2002

Furthermore, the Red-Green government pushed for 73 Airbus military aircraft A400 at 250 m EUR each, totalling 8.5 billion EUR.[8] Worldwide, all defense budgets increased in 2001 and 2002. According to the Financial Times, in 2001, weapons were bought for 804 billion USD, while 50 per cent of the exports came from the U.S., 17.4 per cent from Great Britain. The largest amount of weapons have been sent to crisis regions in the Middle East, (40 per cent), of which Saudi Arabia received the largest portion, 7.3 per cent. How cynical it is to first sell our weapons to those countrs and then send our soldiers as "peacekeepers" there.

Also, the EADS made some significant profit in 2002 (1.44 billion EUR), a fifth more than in the previous year. Especially after the federal elections, 22nd September, 2002, EADS expected that the re-elected government of Schröder and Fischer would push through the A 400M order, which they did, although the government at the same time always claims to have no funds left in their budget.

But with the looming Iraq crisis and the prospects of war in their minds, the "Social Democrats" and "Green pacifists" vowed to further help the weapons industry. In the U.S. the Pentagon and the military industrial complex confirmed closer cooperation.[9] Stocks of Lockheed-Martin, Raytheon, General Dynamics and Northop-Grumman rose by 3 per cent, while other traditional manufacturers stagnated or lost. Profit has been doubled at all the above-mentioned weapons manufacturers, compared with figures from 2001. The defense budget of the U.S. was 331 billion U.S. dollars in 2001, but shall grow up to 451 billion U.S. dollars until 2007. That may show how long ahead the Pentagon and White House, but also the military-industrial complex, plan, and how long they think the Woildwar will last. That's why Bush had to win another 4-year term.

Especially since an U.S. consortium took over Howold Deutsche Werft AG in Kiel, Germany, producing the U31 submarine anxiety in

---

8.   Handelsblatt 13th December 2001)
9.   Handelsblatt 6th September 2002

Europe is at its peak, and Germany but also other European states who together form the European Defense Initiative, increase their military budgets in order to have something to put against American domination, and in order to remain, or better, become independent from the U.S.

Even the German Bundeswehr in their study, "international policy, management of conflicts through military interventions?" stated that "The use of military force by NATO in the Kosovo conflict, without a legitimating UN resolution but on bases of a mandate NATO will issue for itself by defining an unsecure situation, will be the blueprint for military interventions in case of ethnic conflicts in the Caucasian region and Russia in relation to oil resources of the Caspian Sea, where a massive competition has been launched between Western and Russian oil companies, and between Washington and Moscow over strategic interests."[10]

Also, the vice secretary of state in the Clinton administration, Strobe Talbot, said on 11th September, 1997, that, "the resolving of conflicts in the regions must be our task number one, as this is the precondition for exploiting the oil resources."[11]

The U.S. and German-dominated Europe have different interests, and may even stand against each other at some time in the current war. U.S. capital fights German capital. It is New York versus Frankfurt.

The conservative Frankfurter Allgemeine Zeitung for quite a while has advocated the European Defense Initiative and even asked provocantly, "Will we be forever America's junior partner?"[12] and went on to outline the diverging interests between Europe and the U.S. in the Middle East, while also citing what the two blocks had in common: an interest in the "free flow of oil at reasonable prices."

---

10.   Universität der Bundeswehr, Hamburg, August 1998 Pradetto
11.   Wirtschaftswoche 11th September 1997
12.   Frankfurter Allgemeine Zeitung (FAZ) 15th May 1999

But it is not only Germans who want to be able to rival the U.S. The French defense minister demanded increasing military spending in order to "build up an efficient European military industry."[13] as well.

2. Rich & Poor in Germany:

While in the late nineties Germany accounted for an annual growth of 2.8 per cent, we see the country now in recession, with a prospect of deflationary developments as we have witnessed in Japan for more than a decade. In 1998, private comsumption rose by 1.7 per cent, public spending by modest 0.5 per cent, inflation by 1 per cent, and wages nominally (!) were increased by 1.5 per cent, but in effect they shrank, compared to the rise in productivity. While productivity since 1983 rose by almost 40 per cent, the level of wages today are tumbling at the level of 1980 (!!), clear of inflation. At the same time, the average net income of entrepreneurs and major corporations grew at the proud rate of 9 per cent. One could say that we could either work 40 per cent less than in 1980, but have the same purchasing power, meaning the same wages inlcuding the normal inflation, or have 40 per cent more in our pockets while working as hard as in the eighties, without taking a single cent from the shareholder's value. In other words: the investor or entre-preneur who invested in a production twenty years ago did get a good return on investment then, and he would get it now as well, even if we worked 40 per cent less and got the same payment as in 1983, or if we were paid 40 per cent more but worked as much as we did back then. The rise in productivity makes this miracle possible. From 1980 until 1997, productivity rose by 35 per cent,; from 1991 until 1997 alone it has been 18 per cent; in 1997 a marvelous 3.7 per cent. While the media in Germany *unisono* declared war on the social system in post-war Germany and in the East, citing it inaffordable, poductivity rose steadily. No one can explain why we had been so rich in the years before that we could afford a good health care, pension and social sys-

---

13. Frankfurter Allgemeine Zeitung (FAZ) 18th June 1999

tem, but now that productivity rose, the income of people on the payroll shrank every year. We should be richer and not poorer than the people of the 1980s, as we have been working harder and more efficiently.

So how is it possible to make people work harder or become more efficient and productive and pay them less every year? It is possible only through disinformation campaigns, in other words, propaganda. Since the fall of the Berlin wall in 1989 there has been one big lie being told over and over again by nearly all newspapers in East and West Germany and throughout Europe. The lie was that the social systems were cracking down because they have become too expensive and overweighed, inaffordable in other words. We were told by our TV stations and other propaganda media, preaching neo-liberal nonesense, that we were living on the next generation's expenses, that our health system was good but not efficient, and therefore too expensive, that we had too many people accounting for unemployment benefits or social security and too many pensioners because there were ever more older people than young people in our country.

But is this really true? The federal statistics office in Wiesbaden as well as the German Bundesbank in Frankfurt regularly publish pretty accurate figures showing the opposite:

The share of social security expenses in Germany's GNP in 1975 was exactly 34 per cent; in 1994 it was at 33.3 per cent; in 1997 at 34.4 per cent, and since then it has fallen steadily, although there are more people relying on it. This means that over the past quarter of a century we had a very constant social expenditure. It did not become overweight at all. In fact, more people relying on social security but sharing the same quota means effectively that the single applicant for social welfare in 1997 got less than a person in 1975 got, although, I have to repeat myself, productivity rose in the meantime and should have made us all, employees, entrepreneurs and investors, richer, but also our communities who pay for the social welfare of those who are unable to work or simply don't find work anymore. The lie of the exploding social welfare system spread only because all the mass media in Germany repeated it often enough and because many hard-working Germans wanted to believe it. They wanted to believe that foreigners are responsible for the crisis, but even if there were a crisis, it had certainly not been foreigners to blame, but those who claimed the rise of productivity acchieved by employees, investors and entrepreneurs for themselves alone. Most of these shareholders didn't even pay the taxes they owed to our state. However, those are the ones who speak of people relying on social welfare or unemployment benefits as parasites. The same big lie has been employed by the Schröder/Fischer government in order to justify destruction of the health care system. British Prime Minister Tony Blair has done the same in Britain with the NHS and ruined the system by citing inefficiencies and waste of money, while the Tories under Margaret Thatcher would not have dared to go as far as the "New Labor" government did. The British public became aware that Blair was neither doing anything new nor anything in the tradition of the Labor party, but had committed his government to old conservatism. The share of the health care costs of Germany's GNP in 1980 was 6.1 per cent, according to the federal statistical bureau in Wiesbaden. In 1995 in West Germany it was 6.5 per cent, and in all of Germany, 6.9 per cent, where it has remained pretty constant until now, so there is no such explosion of healh care cost as the neo-liberal politicians in SPD and the Green party want to make us believe. Instead, as the conservative financial paper Handelsblatt[14] writes, the DAX-listed thirty biggest and richest major corporations benefit from Schröder's reform "Agenda 2010," since labour costs shrank significantly after the Social Democrats' crackdown on those health care, social security and pension benefits other Social Democrats and Unions had fought for a hundred years ago. Handelsblatt[15] asserts that never before in the past thirty years has there been a more ruthless

---

14. 27th August 2003 Dax-Werte profitieren von Reformen/DAX profits from reforms
15. 27th August 2003

sucking on the insured than under the coalition government of Schröder. His health reform, the paper says, now requires employees to pay for their health care, whereas it used to be a burden shared between employer and employee. The classical model Social Democrats once fought for under Bismarck is dead now. It has been killed by today's "Social Democrats" who employed a manager of VW, Hartz, to orchestrate the reform of the labour market in Germany and who had been laurated and applaused by the German media, from fairly liberal if not left leaning papers such as "Frankfurter Rundschau", SPIEGEL magazine, "Süddeutsche Zeitung" to those right-wing daily circulations of the Springer publishing group including Die WELT but also tabloids like BILD Zeitung. The hype these journalists created in favour of these reforms can be compared with what Goebbels managed to create in the "Third Reich". The name of this manager, Hartz, became a synonym for an unprecedented crackdown on what once has been admired as the West-German system of a social free market. It has all been destructed within a few months.

The same applies to the pension system, whose share in the GNP in 1980 was 8.8 per cent; in 1995 in West Germany 8.5 per cent, and in all of Germany 9.7 per cent, and remained constant until now. Nevertheless, the Schröder/Fischer government and mass media tell us lies about the explosion of costs and the inaffordable system, the burdens of which fewer working young people are said to carry on their shoulders for ever more old people.

At first sight it sounds logical, given the fact that, due to the marvelous health care system, Germany used to have more and more people live longer, while there was a steady decline in Germany's birth rate. In the nineties, productivity rose annually by 2.5 per cent. The number of pensioners instead will grow between 2000 and 2040, only by 0.75 per cent per annum. In other terms, the populistic approach of mass media and politicians, suggesting that we won't be able to afford a good pension system any longer is nothing but an impertinent lie, and seeks to play the elder generation against the younger, and thus undermine the pillars of the solidarity systems, the socalled "treaty of the generations". It also does not take into account, however, that the German population has accumulated ever more wealth and is benefitting from a steadily rising productivity. No matter how old a person is, per capita there is more to distribute than ever before. Whether a "capita" is eight, eighteen or eighty years old, per capita we are getting richer and richer. The only problem is, of course, the distribution of this wealth. Also, while our economy becomes more and more productive, meaning we are able to produce more by using less energy and labour in less time, this would mean that we all could be richer, and not only statistically per capita, but in real terms as well. The income is distributed as follows: In 1980 almost a quarter of the GDP resulted from entrepreneurship and shareholder values, while in 1997 it was closer to 40 per cent and today makes almost half of the GDP, while the payroll in 1980 accounted for more than half of the GDP and dropped to merely 40 per cent in 1997, and today is just above 35 per cent. Social welfare, pensions and unemployment benefits remained steady at 26.3 per cent since 1980. The net income of all private households rose between 1991 and 1997 alone by 26 per cent. This figure sounds wonderful, but a closer scrutiny reveals that the top 10 per cent of German society became incredibly rich, while the majority of employees had to accept that their net income shrank by 7 per cent following years in which they were told by the media as well as politicians and shareholders that due to down-sizing and economic stagnation no pay increases would be possible without risking jobs in all major indsutries. At the same time, of course, gross return on investment jumped into orbit, hitting 43 per cent, and leading to German corporations piling up incredible cash reserves in 1998 of 237.4 billion Deutsche Mark, which has been a historic record. German Labor Minister Riester admitted in Frankfurter Allgemeine Zeitung that there has been a spread between incomes.[16]

---

16.   Frankfurter Allgemeine Zeitung (FAZ) 26th March 1999

The fairy tale of entrepreneurs using those savings in order to invest into new technologies, inventions and new jobs was a blunt lie, as the number of employees shrank by 1.4 million between 1993 and 1997. Above all, four fifths of newly created wealth stems from interest payments and dividends from financial markets. Needless to say, none of these "investments" in stocks, shares or derivatives has ever created or even saved one single job. The German trade unions, DGB, warned in 2000 that the net purchasing power of the average employee since 1980 rose by mere 4.3 per cent, while the real income of the corporations grew by 84.4 per cent in the past twenty years.

All this would make sense if there had not been this tremendous rise in productivity of more than 40 per cent in the past twenty years, which should justify a strenghtening of the purchasing power and should also make it affordable for us to have a proper social system.

Of course, investors today invest considerably more money than in the eighties in order to accumulate the same profit, but that is a mere financial question in relation to the capitalistic principles our world still follows, and it is a problem of its system, not a problem of the so-called capital coefficient. So why would workers in Germany and other industrialised nations agree to waive their rights in sharing the benefits of the rise of productivity, which they have achieved commonly with the investors and the entrepreneur who invested in new technologies and inventions? So far, the rise of productivity went only into the pockets of the shareholders, although it would be legitimate and fair to share it between workers, investors and entrepreneurs. Seen from the shareholder's point of view, it would also make sense, as wages reflecting the rise of productivity also guarantee a higher purchasing power, which would fuel the economy and spark new growth by continuing demand. It should be in the self-interest of any sober thinking investor and entrepreneur, but somehow our present economic system deludes the other way. It leads us to think that we can have profits of 15, 20 or 30 per cent per annum, but we forget to ask the question: where does this profit come from if our annual growth rates are below 2 per cent?

One does not have to be an economist to understand that the profit maximisation dreams of the nineties were unreal and that such artificial growth can not go on forever, but that the big bubble will burst. In Germany the so-called "Neue Markt" has been shut down just recently. It should never have existed, we know today.

How rich are we?

The Frankfurter Allgemeine Zeitung[17] asserted in 1999 that from 1990 until 1998 more than 2,000 billion Deutsche Mark have been accumulated by private households in Germany. In 1998 alone it was a record of 263 billion DM. The total wealth of private housholds in Germany at the end of 1998 was 5,600 billion DM. The average savings of a single household in Germany was 153,000 DM. These are impressive figures, but how have these been distributed between rich and poor? The lower classes, as in any "free democracy," saved less or nothing. The lowest 10 per cent in Germany had an average of 11,000 DM in debts; the richest 1 per cent of the households accounted for 30 per cent of the nation's wealth. The top 10 per cent had a share of 50% Per cent We are of course not a socialist system, so I would not really question this if we all had equal chances to accumulate such wealth by hard work. But more and more of us ordinary citizens are excluded from social life, and it's getting harder every day to find work or open a business. Also, one has to acknowledge the fact that none of the super rich have ever accumulated their wealth by hard work, but by letting others work for them, inherit from an old aunt, or by speculation. The later especially has become increasingly popular in the nineties, when (as in the twenties of the last century) a mass-media campaign promoted buying stocks. While there has been some kind of hysteria about the stock market, and especially the so-called "Neue Markt," and everyone not holding stocks must have felt stupid, the mere facts speak a different language. Ninety-three per cent of Germany's population

17.   27th October 1999

above 14 years of age did not own one single stock. Only 4.1 million privateers in 1997 owned stocks, while the richest 1 per cent of our society controled more than 70 per cent of the stocks and shares. In Germany we can be proud of 85 billionaires and 131,000 millionaires. The top ten thousand Germans account for 28 per cent of all wealth in Germany. Four-fifths of the newly generated wealth results from dividends from stocks and shares and interest. From 1991 until 1997 alone their income rose by 26 per cent to 220 billion Deutsche Mark. The German statistical office, which said it won't do any more such surveys (one should ask why not!), admitted that they probably know only of 40 per cent of the real figure, as much will be tax-evaded anyhow. So we know who is holding such partly state-guaranteed treasury bonds in Luxembourg, Liechtenstein and Switzerland. The German state is stupid enough to pay a guaranteed interest to those who by their tax evasion only forced the state to issue treasury bonds.

Knowing all these facts makes it simply impossible to explain why, while we have become richer and richer, per capita only of course, more and more efficient and flexible, but seem to be unable to enjoy the fruits of our hard work, even lose jobs although there would be enough work for all if we only consider the state our child care, educational and public service systems are in, not to speak of many old people not being treated well in nursing homes. There is only one simple and unpleseant answer: Some parasites are stealing from us. Let's have a look at who, apart from the privateers mentioned above, it might be:

Who's getting the rosins of the pie?

The federal government, in its attempt to reduce unemployment in East Germany, subsidized such "poor" corporations as VW, Opel, Siemens Dow Chemical, and granted them wide-ranging tax relief. One could applaud the government for such actions if the jobs being created really had been there for a long term, but most of these jobs disappeared pretty soon. No other EU country has ever seen such a number of subsidies go to the major indsutries as Germany. As the institute of economics (DIW) asserted in a study, in 1994 only 91 billion Deutsche Mark had been paid in corporate taxes, while 132 billion Deutsche Mark had been transferred by the state as subsidies. In essence, german industry got more of taxpayer's money than they paid in taxes. Also, on the European level, German taxpayers compensated such major corporations as Sabena and Swissair with hundreds of millions of Euros,[18] as these airlines' acquisitions of Airbus passenger aircraft had been secured by Hermes government bonds.

Also, Daimler-Chrysler was subsidized by 57 million €, 31 per cent of their intended investment in a new plant in Kölleda, Thuringia, and BMW received significant amounts again and again for their plant in Leipzig, Saxony, all our taxpayer's money. The EU seeks to reduce such direct government involvement, as it is the body's over-all strategy to exclude public involvements in the long term.[19] Anyhow, it appears akward that those major corporations always seek to blame the state for "over regulating" businesses, and therefore want to limit its influence, at the same time demanding financial engagement, and when profitable, avoid taxes. Daimler-Chrysler didn't pay any corporate taxes, even three years before the merger, although they had double-digit billions of Deutsche Mark profits. During the late nineties, multinational corporations like Siemens made huge profits, i.e. in 1999 a third more—after tax.[20] And in 2000, the same corporation had a profit before taxes of 2 billion Deutsche Mark, but after declaring taxes they had 5 billion Deutsche Mark on their balance sheets. "Daimler-Chrysler AG increased its profit in 1999 by 15 per cent, up to 7.6 billion Deutsche Mark, and Deutsche Bank AG had profited tremendously from acquisition of Bankers Trust, which gave them a boost of a record net profit increase by 42.6 per cent (1.88 billion €), while at the same time Deutsche Bank AG was able to reduce its tax liability by 39 per cent, down to 848 million €."[21] BMW does not pay any more cor-

18.   Handelsblatt 28th January 2001
19.   Neues Deutschland (ND) 12th February 2002
20.   Frankfurter Allgemeine Zeitung 4th November 1999

porate taxes, since they burnt their fingers with their ROVER engagement. After they sold ROVER they were well-off again, but that does not mean that they returned to the practice of paying taxes. Bayer AG uses a similar excuse, citing the Lipobay desaster as their reason not to pay corporate taxes in six west German cities. Daimler-Chrysler excuses itself by saying they lost money when taking over Chrysler. Nevertheless, their letters to shareholders speak of the most successful year since founding of the company. Companies like these use "additional possibilities not to pay taxes, despite billions of € profit."[22]

Well, how did these companies use their profits, which they were be able to accumulate only because of their market dominance and a business- friendly government? Have they, as one usually hears from neoliberal politicians, invested in new technologies, education, job creation, in our future? Far from that. As said above, four-fifths of the newly accumulated wealth in Germany stems from dividends, shareholder value and interests, not from genuine investments.

From the mid-nineties on, gains made from production increasingly went onto the financial markets and not back into production or into new inventions. In 1997, 31.5 per cent of profits have been placed on the financial markets in order to accumulate money with money. In 1998, it was already 37.5 per cent, and now it is above 46 per cent. When money is drawn out of production because money makes more money with money than labor, it kills, not creates, jobs. During the years before 1997 it was always much less than 30 per cent. Investments in equipment or new technologies in 1998 increased only by 5 per cent. The absolute figure of employees rose only by 0.3 per cent. From 1991 until 1995 the tax burden of the employees rose by 31.5 per cent, while the entrepreneurs benefitted from 13.7 per cent reduction in taxes. In 1998, the over-all rise in the absolute figure for corpo-

21.   Westfälische Allgemeine Zeitung (WAZ) 27th October 1999
22.   Wirtschaftswoche 7th February 2002

rate tax has been 4.5 per cent, while the over-all profits for corporations grew by 14 per cent.

The formerly completely state-owned railway company, Deutsche Bahn AG (DB), still is on breastfeeding by the state, but denies any profit participation. Since being privatised in the early nineties, DB received billions of € in government aid while laying off thousands of workers and reducing their service to the minimum and most profitable long-range inter-city and inter-city express trains.[23] When Schröder's "Red-Green" coalition government announced their new tax 'reform' plans in 2000, promising a tax relief of 80 billion € from 2005, shareholders and managers of major corporations in Germany opend the champagne bottles. The corporate tax shrank to only 25 per cent, gains from selling shares are now tax free. Experts and analysts calculated this tax gift to banks and insurance groups, as well as holdings, to be worth a double-digit billion € amount.[24] Even before Schröder acted as Santa Claus, Deutsche Bank AG was able to legally reduce its spending in taxes by 41 per cent, while increasing its profit in the same year by 39 per cent. One can also say that we, the taxpayers, pay for the gains of Deutsche Bank AG and their shareholders. We could also give our money directly to them. Why bother with a state as an intermediary? Because of Schröder's tax reform, Deutsche Bank AG was able to sell its Allianz AG shares tax free and keep another 7 billion € in its books.[25] The estimated tax relief major corporations benefit from is tremendous, i.e. for Allinaz AG it is 25 billion €, for Deutsche Bank AG 18 billion €, for Münchner Rückversicherung 10 billion €.[26] The effects these legal tax evasions had were described by an article in 'Der Spiegel' magazine,[27] which claimed that cities, towns and

---

23.   Handelsblatt 19th February 2003
24.   Frankfurter Allgemeine Zeitung (FAZ) 9th February 2000
25.   Frankfurter Allgemeine Zeitung (FAZ) 7th June 2000
26.   ISW Wirtschaftsinfo Nr. 32/2000 & Manager Magazin
27.   DER SPIEGEL No. 35/2001 "Germany's cities face collaps"

communities in Germany suffer from the new tax reform, allowing corporations to avoid the corporate tax by simply founding a foreign corporation. Although a company like Bayer AG employes thousands and produces in Leverkusen near Cologne, the city of Leverkusen, once relatively well-off, all of a sudden didn't see a single cent from Bayer AG, as the global player, like many others under the new legislation, had various possibilities to reduce its corporate taxes to zero. Even a city like Frankfurt am Main, the financial center of Germany and Europe, all of a sudden had to deal with a tax default of approximately 500 million €, although all the banks, insurance companies and financial service industries reside in skyscrapers and turn around multi-billions every day. A new special clause in Schröder's tax reform allows global players not only to negotiate their taxes, but also compensate their losses in one business field with gains in others, even if these are legally separate business entities. This has been a major advantage for insurers like Allianz AG and others, who just for this purpose start seperating their business and form single units so that fiscally, no taxes apply at all. E-on, i.e. was able to make a 5.4 billion Deutsche Mark profit, but requested money back from taxes paid in earlier years under the new law.

As in Germany, cities and communities receive the corporate tax but also have to meet their obligations to pay for social welfare, the new tax reform drastically reduced their financial abilities, so that they cried out to the federal government, which reacted by taking on obligations for social welfare and unemployment benefits, but combined these traditionally different allowances and limited these to the absolute minimum, blaming empty pockets. And these fiscal pockets were empty, of course, but whose fault has this been?

The financially disastrous tax reform becomes evident in an article by 'Handelsblatt,' headlined "Major corporations get tax refund,"[28] in which the financial paper asserts that before the tax reform the state

---

28.   Handelsblatt 17th January 2002 "Großkonzerne erhalten Steuern zurück"

received over-all 23.6 billion € (2000) from corporate taxes and in 2001 only 1.7 billion €.

And the Frankfurter Allgemeine Zeitung jubilantly celebrated the billions from the minister in Berlin. "Allianz acchieved 3.4 billion € extra profit due to tax reduction,"[29] and in 2002 they realized another 2.5 billion €, as they could sell-off shares they held in other corporations tax-free, while the shares of non-profitable companies could be deducted from taxes. So as we know now who is profiting from the 'Socialdemocratic-Green' government's tax reform, we should have a look at those who still pay taxes:

From 1992 until 1997, the state's income from corporate taxes shrank by 15 per cent, while the income from payroll taxes increased by 21 per cent, and from VAT by 22 per cent. The development in the past forty years shows that increasingly, employees have to compensate for the corporation's failure or unwillingness to contribute to our society. While in 1960 the share of the taxes paid by employees was 12 per cent of the total fiscal income of the state, in 1996 it was 36 per cent, and now it is closer to 42 per cent. It is slowing down only because of an increasing unemployment. For the same time, the share of taxes being paid by entrepreneurs accounted for 16 per cent, and in 1996 for only 5 per cent. Now, after the tax reform, it is nearing zero, and in some cases even becomes a negative tax balance. The corporate tax in 1985 still brought 7.3 per cent into the state's wallet; in 1996 it was mere 3.4 per cent, while the VAT makes more than three times what all corporate taxes and corporate income taxes ever made. From 1999 until 2002, payroll taxes accounted for a share increase in the national tax burden of 2.4 per cent and amounted to 68 billion €, while all corporate income taxes together shrank by 20 per cent within the same three years, and now only make 29 billion €. The share of VAT in the

---

29. Frankfurter Allgemeine Zeitung (FAZ) 15th February 2001 "Allianz erhielt durch Steuerersparnis 3,4 Milliarden € Überschuß"

overall tax income of Germany rose by 9 per cent from 1999 until 2002.[30]

The German Bundesbank, in its statistical monthly report, cited a first-time-ever complete disappearance of income from corporate tax,while the normal income tax dropped by 39 per cent.[31]

In other words: because corporations are benefitting from tax reliefs and the new tax legislation, we, the ordinary taxpayers, have to make up for the difference by having more deductions than ever on our pay statements, and when buying any kind of goods with the little money we still may have in our pockets.

This is the reason for the financial crisis our country is in, and it is also the reason for the mental crisis and lack of motivation our society evidently suffers from.

How poor are we?

"Poor people are more often sick and die earlier," states the conservative daily Frankfurter Allgemeine Zeitung (FAZ),[32] and continues quoting scientific research into heart diseases and the potenial reasons for such. "People with lower income face a two-to-three-times higher risk of strokes and heart attacks than people with normal income. Children of unemployed people are more often sick as well." The same paper, really not known for a left-leaning or even socialist editorial position, claimed in an earlier edition that, "the number of poor people in Germany grew significantly."[33] According to this article, 12.7 per cent of households in Germany live below the poverty line, 32.4 per cent of single mothers are considered poor, as the federal statistics office asserted. More than a third of all Germans are unable to afford a

---

30. Frankfurter Rundschau (FR) 21st November 2001 "Arbeitnehmer Anteil an Steuerlast nimmt zu"
31. German Bundesbank, monthly report Nr. 2/2002 (Monatsbericht der Bundesbank Nr.2, Statist. Teil, S.54)
32. Frankfurter Allgemeine Zeitung (FAZ) 25th March 1999
33. Frankfurter Allgemeine Zeitung (FAZ) 01st December 1999

private pension plan, a quarter of Germans are unable to save even 50 € per month. Forty-four per cent can not afford dental care, 20 per cent can't spend their holidays abroad, 55 per cent of the children of poor families never reach secondary school or even college, not to speak of universities. What a stupid system, to exclude young people regardless of their intelligence, simply because their parents are not doing well. The FAZ goes on, saying that "poorer children in many cases are not fed well."

One million children in Germany are living on social welfare.

A significant figure is also to be seen at court-ordered reposessions and auctions. From 1997 until 2001 the figure doubled, and is high as ever before.[34] Also never seen before in Germany was the number of people sleeping on the street. Five hundred and forty thousand people are considered homeless. The fact that the West German government after unification sold off one million flats, for often symbolic prices, to "investors" who tore down the certainly not nice, mass buildings in the former East, is a slap in the face for people who are in need of an affordable apartement today. Not only do people who were laid off suffer under the present regime, but medium-sized and small entrepreneurs as well. In the first quarter of the year 2001, an increase of insolvencies by 20 per cent was reported, compared to the year before. More than 100,000 employees were laid off.[35] One of the reasons responsible was the economic downturn, but another is the declining willingness of banks to grant loans to businesses.[36]

According to a study by the University of Marburg, more than five million people in Germany live under the poverty line. They live on less than 5 € per day for food, and have a seven-year lower life expectancy.[37] And more than 2.8 million people in Germany live in a covered-up poverty, but are not counted by the regular statistics, as their

34. DIE WELT, 20th November 2001
35. Süddeutsche Zeitung (SZ) 13th October 2001
36. DIE WELT, 27th June 2001
37. Neues Deutschland (ND) 4th December 1999, Studie der Universität Marburg

income may be as low as the social welfare to which they would not be entitled as they still may have work. It appears that for every hundred people relying on social welfare, there are 110 who fall through any social net.[38] Especially under the red-green government, the number of children living in poverty has increased, says a study by the National Conference on Poverty, according to which more than 1.1 million children in 2001 lived below the poverty line, whereas it had been 700,000 in 1994.[39] "Every seventh child in Germany is raised in poverty," headlined even the conservative FAZ, quoting from a social welfare organization that, "they come to kindergarden or school wihtout breakfast, are more often sick because of unsufficient feeding, can't participate in extra-curricular activities, and have less chances for their future."[40] But people still working increasingly also are seen as poor. The federal government's report on rich and poor acknowledged a widening gap between rich and poor, saying that in 1998, 1.1 million households enjoyed an income above 65,000 €, whereas every fifth has less than 60 per cent of the average income of 30,000 € (before taxes). According to this report by the German labor ministry, the number of people who, despite having a job, are considered poor rose between 1994 and 1998 from 38 per cent to 44 per cent.[41] "Households with children have less to spend," headlined the Handelsblatt, referring to a report by the DIW, according to which single mothers face poverty.[42]

The above facts are nothing else but a declaration of bankruptcy in our political and economic system. A society in which children become a poverty risk won't reproduce itself. It becomes cold and lonely. The disappointment of people with a system that provides no security, because only the shareholder value counts, will provoke anger and

---

38. Frankfurter Allgemeine Zeitung (FAZ) 22nd April 1998
39. Deutscher Depeschen Dienst (ddp) 27th June 2001
40. Frankfurter Allgemeine Zeitung (FAZ) 26th October 2000
41. Neues Deutschland (ND) 4th November 2000 (Armuts- & Reichtumsbericht des Bundesarbeitsministeriums)
42. Handelsblatt 8th August 2002 (Wochenbericht des DIW)

hatred. The so-called "Red-Green" coalition is proud to claim that it is in power, but it is only in government. Even as a government it is only transitional, but does a lot of harm to our democratic system.

Our state is in a crisis. Our society is in a crisis. The crisis is an economical, political and cultural one. Our system does not work anymore. It has been the victim of exploitation by the rich, not the poor. While we should be richer than ever before, because we have worked hard to acchieve an ever higher productivity, some parasites bribe and blackmail our politicians to change legislation the way they need it in order to make it look legal, although it will never be legitimate. Unless we question the legitimacy of the present system, we will in a short while be confronted with a right-wing populist who may lead us into a future that we had believed was our country's dark past. To say that because I am able to voice my criticism proves that I am wrong, is the threat of fascism.

Article 20 of the basic Law, our constitution, states that "the Federal Republic of Germany is a *social, federal, state* based on the rule of law. The legislation is bound by the constitution, the judicative branch by the law and the executive branch by legislation. The German people have the right of resistance against whoever intends to abolish these principles."

Given the fact that Schröder is running amok through the social net with a chain saw in his hand, while he commits himself to exactly the same economic policy Reich's Chancellor Brüning employed, and that the world is in a crisis worse than in 1929, does not leave us much time to prevent the worst.

I would prefer to not see it become necessary to invoke Article 20 of our constitution.

0-595-29552-5